Interpreting Hashtag Politics

Interpreting Hashtag Politics

Policy Ideas in an Era of Social Media

Stephen Jeffares
Lecturer, School of Government and Society, University of Birmingham, UK

First published 2014 by
PALGRAVE MACMILLAN

Palgrave Macmillan in the UK is an imprint of Macmillan Publishers Limited, registered in England, company number 785998, of Houndmills, Basingstoke, Hampshire RG21 6XS.

Palgrave Macmillan in the US is a division of St Martin's Press LLC, 175 Fifth Avenue, New York, NY 10010.

Palgrave Macmillan is the global academic imprint of the above companies and has companies and representatives throughout the world.

Palgrave® and Macmillan® are registered trademarks in the United States, the United Kingdom, Europe and other countries.

ISBN 978–1–137–35773–1

This book is printed on paper suitable for recycling and made from fully managed and sustained forest sources. Logging, pulping and manufacturing processes are expected to conform to the environmental regulations of the country of origin.

A catalogue record for this book is available from the British Library.

A catalog record for this book is available from the Library of Congress.

Transferred to Digital Printing in 2014

To my mum, Lis

Contents

Figures and Tables

Figures

Tables

Preface and Acknowledgements

This book is about public policy in an era of social media, internet enabled smart phones, tablet computers and digital availability of everything everywhere. It considers the implications of these technologies for how policy actors communicate their messages. Soon after their arrival social media and networking platforms, such as Twitter but also Tumblr, Facebook, Google+ and Pinterest, began to use the hash symbol (known in some countries as the pound sign '#') to tag posts, in order to make them searchable or express sentiment in their messages. While this book discusses examples of policy-related hashtags in use, by 'hashtag politics' I refer to something deeper, something that has been developing over recent years and something that is coming to fruition.

Hashtag politics is a shift towards the purposive and careful naming of a policy idea or specific initiative. It is the formation of a policy idea, with instrumental intent and brand-like consistency. Just as a hashtag on Twitter brackets a discussion and gives it a boundary and a focus for that discussion, hashtag politics does the same. The starting point for this book was a puzzle of how the creation of a distinct policy idea helps to communicate and convey a broader political project of intent, actions and practices, and yet also creates a space for contestation and critique. My hunch going into this project was that policy ideas were about policy actors adapting to the possibilities and the challenges of the day. They have at their disposal mechanisms for broadcasting to millions of followers and friends and attracting the attention of online and print journalism. And yet all of these places, platforms and channels and sources of information and interaction also create a busy and congested space where policy actors and their ideas compete for attention. In response, policy actors are branding their activities with policy ideas. More recently we see them adopting digital technology to communicate these policy ideas, but in many respects this is of secondary concern. More important is that such tools would be of little use if policy actors had not begun to adapt their practices.

My first exposure to hashtag politics came through a case study during the course of my research of policy-making in Birmingham, UK, during which a policy idea called 'Flourishing Neighbourhoods' seemed to be used by a wide range of policy actors in the city, while its ownership and origins were contested (Jeffares, 2008). Something I did not get a chance to explore fully was the curious and somewhat rapid demise and spectacular death of this policy idea. Whilst a change of political administration offered a straightforward explanation, I was left with a sense that something more was going on. In subsequent projects I remained attuned to the role of policy ideas. In work with Chris Skelcher, Helen Sullivan and Michael Farrelly, I encountered first-hand the policy ideas of an 'Integrated Copenhagen' and 'City Citizenship' in Rotterdam (Skelcher et al., 2013). Similarly, with Martin Willis, we set out to understand how local actors give meaning to a centrally formulated policy idea, in this case an initiative called 'Total Place' (Willis & Jeffares, 2011). Finally, working with Helen Dickinson, Jon Glasby, Helen Sullivan, Suzanne Robinson, Greg Hughes and Alyson Nicholds, I explored how a range of professionals in health service and social care agencies understood the idea of Joint Commissioning, and subsequently Integrated Care (Dickinson et al., 2013). The common denominator of the three projects was a method called Q methodology, developed to systematically measure subjective views and offering a means of identifying shared viewpoints.

This book is an attempt to bring together my thinking over the last few years and projects, to develop a definition of policy ideas and to explore the practice of hashtag politics. The book draws on the fruits of three academic communities. First, it draws on the work of interpretive policy studies, and is inspired by Maarten Hajer, Dvora Yanow, Frank Fischer, Henk Wagenaar, Merlijn van Hulst, Nick Mahony, Janet Newman and in particular the work around political discourse of Ernesto Lacalu and Chantel Mouffe, conveyed by Steven Griggs, David Howarth, Jacob Torfing, Eva Sorensen, Aletta Norvel and Jason Glyos. It is this interpretive and discursive work that grounds and gives foundation to what I infer by hashtag politics and I am thankful and grateful to all those who have guided, questioned and commented along the way.

The second community to note here is Q methodology, an interdisciplinary community of scholars and practitioners who share an interest in measuring and mapping shared or inter-subjectivity, guided by the work of psychologist Dr William Stephenson (1902–1989). The sign of a good academic community is that it nurtures newcomers, offers support and guidance and tools to design, administer, analyse, interpret and publish research. The Q methodology that features in this book is inspired, supported and challenged by Steven R Brown, Rachel Baker, Helen Mason, Job van Exel, Gjalt de Graaf, Amanda Wolf, Klara Overland, Dan Thomas, Jim Rhodes, Peter Schmolck, Eefje Cuppen, Simon Watts, Tim Deignan and the students of workshops in

Amsterdam, Essex, De Montford and students of my Q method class at the University of Birmingham.

The third community that informed and inspired this work is perhaps best labelled as Online Text Analytics. It started with a workshop chaired by Rachel Gibson at the University of Manchester where Dr Stuart Shulman presented his work developing a methodology for analysing digital text. It exposed me to a new and exciting world of text and online analysis and to a growing community of scholars who are interested in the messy and sometimes daunting task of understanding the meaning of anything from a single tweet to a dataset of a million. Shulman's tool DiscoverText offered me the means to capture, code and classify social media posts on a myriad of policy ideas, and a grant from the British Academy (SG112101) allowed me to employ a team of researchers to explore how policy actors and the wider public interact and modify policy ideas, and how meaning develops, crystallises or changes over time. An additional grant from the University of Birmingham trans-Atlantic travel fund enabled me to visit and learn from colleagues at the UIC Health Media Collaboratory – Sherry Emery, Glen Szczpka, Eman Aly and Rachel Kornfield. The possibility of capturing and interpreting these fluid and rapid data was the missing part of the puzzle. When I first started to wonder about policy ideas, Twitter hadn't yet been invented. Twitter and the like has not so much changed how policy actors do policy, but rather it has contributed to its evolution towards something I call hashtag politics.

I am grateful and thankful to everybody listed above, and so many more who have helped, challenged and supported me in pulling together these strands. Particular thanks are due to the anonymous reviewers, Amber Stone-Galilee, Andrew Baird, Steven Kennedy and everybody at Palgrave Macmillan who supported me through the process, as well as Chris Skelcher, Helen Dickinson, Peter John, Helen Sullivan and Steven R Brown for their extensive comments on earlier drafts. Mistakes are my own. This book was conceived and written while Roberts Research Fellow at the University of Birmingham and I am thankful to Catherine Staite and colleagues at INLOGOV for giving me the space and support I needed to get this project finished. Thank you to all my research assistants who coded, questioned and critiqued my ideas: Gill Plumridge, Becky O'Neil, Tom Daniels, Pete Redford, Phoebe Mau, Diha Mulla, Misfa Begum and Sarah Jeffries. I want to express thanks to Martin Willis, and Taylor & Francis and the editors of *Local Government Studies* for permission to draw on the article Willis, M. & Jeffares, S. (2012). 'Four viewpoints of whole area public partnerships.'

Local Government Studies, 38(5), 539–556 in Chapter 4. I want to thank Helen Sullivan for nurturing me through this project since the very beginning, and Steven Griggs for introducing me to the world of critical policy studies. Above all I want to thank Annie Austin for supporting me through the sometimes turbulent times of writing a book, giving me the encouragement to keep going, transforming what was sometimes unintelligible prose by injecting style and grace.

#thankyou

1
Policy Ideas and Hashtag Politics

Hashtag politics is the practice of naming policy ideas, thereby giving them a life and, ultimately, a death. Here are three British examples of hashtag politics:

1. In February 2001, Birmingham City Council adopted 'Flourishing Neighbourhoods' as a strategic priority. During the 12 months of 2002, over 80 different organisations and initiatives aligned with Flourishing Neighbourhoods. In October 2004, questions were asked in the council chamber about why Flourishing Neighbourhoods had been 'scrapped'.
2. In April 2009, the British Government announced an initiative called Total Place, designed to examine public spending and local leadership. In February 2010, Sir Michael Bichard published his report on the 13 official pilot projects and related activity across the country. In December 2011, the Coalition Government were said to have 'torn up Labour's Total Place programme'.
3. In November 2009, soon-to-be Prime Minister David Cameron stated his desire for a 'Big Society'. In UK broadsheet newspapers, 33 articles mentioned the phrase, its merit and related activities. During the 12 months of 2010 this rose to 1,708, growing to 2,293 in 2011 and reducing to 1,377 in 2012 and 680 in 2013. In April 2012, the *Daily Telegraph* suggested the policy idea was 'dead'.

This book is about the practice of creating and discussing policy ideas: those purposive, often branded initiatives of policy-makers, that, in the space of less than a thousand days are coined, fostered, launched, discussed, written about, adopted, critiqued, subverted, derided, ignored, forgotten and replaced. Policy ideas are policy instruments that express deeper ideas, an imagined future couched in a unique, memorable, searchable, branded identity. Despite their taken-for-granted position in policy-making, they are largely overlooked, in contrast to broader political ideas such as 'democracy' or 'neoliberalism'. They are, by some, deemed too narrow to be interesting (Berman, 2009) their visions nebulous, with claims of novelty dismissed as old wine in new bottles; to many they are much-hyped brands that are too easily tarnished. As such, policy actors and researchers ignore them. This book argues that not only are policy ideas worth researching, but that the increasing speed and growing volume of discussion surrounding policy ideas through social media presents a new challenge for both research and policy practice and, therefore, it has never been more important to understand policy ideas.

The widespread adoption of mobile communications and social media channels offers a new environment for policy-making. With social media, never has it been cheaper, easier or quicker to coin and disseminate an idea. Similarly, never has it been easier to expedite the demise of a policy idea, or to mobilise an alternative viewpoint. But also, never has it been easier to ignore a policy idea, amid such noise and information overload.

This book seeks to understand the theory and practice of making policy ideas. Its three aims are to conceptualise policy ideas, to theorise their lifecycle and to understand them in an era of social media. This book provides the first comprehensive conceptualisation of these curious mainstays of policy-making. It offers a new theorisation of the motivation and lifecycle of policy ideas. It draws on a decade of primary empirical research, with examples of policy practice in a range of UK policy initiatives. It shows how our understanding of policy ideas can be illuminated through interviews, observation, policy documents, newspaper archives and social media data.

The book argues that policy ideas are important but underacknowledged tools of modern policy practice. And in an era of social data, where communication is rapid and voluminous, practices and methods are evolving. The book argues that policy ideas are the mechanism by which aspirations, initiatives and projects are expressed. Considerable resources are invested in their development and launch. For policy actors, deciding whether and when to engage or disengage with policy ideas can be a precarious judgement call. Considerable attention is levelled at the latest and loudest. Then the circus moves on and the policy idea is forgotten. Yet despite the centrality of policy ideas in the process of policy-making, current work tends to overlook their importance.

There are several reasons why policy ideas are currently neglected. Political scientists interested in ideas tend to take a macro perspective on broader political ideas. Policy scientists focus on fads and fashions of leadership, rather than specific and, it is argued, narrow and uninteresting programmes or policy instruments. Others seek to understand why agendas take hold during a window of opportunity (Kingdon, 1995). The visions and fantasies expressed in policy ideas designed for broad appeal suggest nebulous managerial jargon and are judged unworthy of detailed study. Policy ideas are associated with the marketisation of political discourse, where selling the message and brand management are more important than the content of the policy (Eshuis & Edwards, 2012; Needham, 2011). The resulting fragmented conceptualisation of policy ideas maps over into how they are understood over time. While most policy ideas are forgotten as quickly as they appeared, when they are reflected upon they are often viewed as old wine in new bottles, or as technical innovations diffusing over time.

The widespread adoption of social media among policy communities means that policy ideas compete for attention and reputation within a voluminous and transient environment, and all the while leaving a digital footprint. The search for this digital footprint finds social scientists, market analysts and computer scientists developing tools to capture, index and visualise, in order to research sentiment, intent and trends. They are seemingly motivated differently: while some wish to predict market fluctuations, others are interested in election outcomes or understanding social mobilisation. So far, efforts to measure the impact of social media on political discourse have relied on crude sentiment meters, designed to cut through the noise to understand the subjectivity of a policy idea.

By highlighting the importance of policy ideas the book explores possibilities for adaptation in the methods and techniques that are used to capture a sense of the fast-moving environment in which policy ideas are communicated. It would be easy for this form of analysis to remain the preserve of IT mavens or quantitative analysts, but this book acknowledges and responds to the argument that it is not enough to simply capture huge 'massified' social media datasets (Neuhaus & Webmoor, 2012); the book explores the possibility of developing techniques to systematically extract subjective expression and evaluate its shape, and develops new methods of understanding the subjective trajectory of the policy idea, its appeal and its eventual demise.

The book investigates how new generations of interpretive policy researchers, ethnographers, discourse theorists, linguists and policy-makers can add real-time subjective analysis of policy ideas to their analytic repertoire. The book speaks to those seeking to go beyond merely separating the signal from the noise and counting it (Silver, 2012). There have recently been calls for a generation of policy actors and researchers who are able to interpret the qualitative aspects of big data (Kim et al., 2013); to that end, this book is offered as one such primer.

This book is based on a decade of research focused on policy ideas, and offers a rich account of published thinking alongside theoretically grounded and methodologically innovative primary research. It draws together disparate literatures to offer a rich conceptualisation of policy ideas, and uses discourse theory to understand their lifecycle. It pulls together literatures on social media from commerce, social movements, electoral politics and professional practice. A particular focus of the book is its methodological offering, including in-depth qualitative analysis, Q methodology and social media text analytics. The arguments draw on rich empirical accounts of policy ideas including the Big Society; Birmingham's Flourishing Neighbourhoods; an idea about area-based budgeting – Total Place; and the 2012 campaign to elect local Police and Crime Commissioners (PCCs), as well as discussion of reforms in nursing (Compassionate Care) and housing benefit (known as the Bedroom Tax).

These British examples are offered to illustrate a broader movement in policy-making globally, whereby policy actors are adapting to the opportunity of new forms of communication and an increasingly congested and multi-platform environment. The thinking in this book is intended to outlive many of the examples herein. It is hoped the concepts and methods it introduces will offer a means for readers to identify examples within their own expertise or locale.

Three challenges for policy ideas

Challenge 1: 'But surely these are not new, we have had policy ideas of the kind you suggest for many years?'

When Franklin D. Roosevelt won the Democratic nomination for the US presidency in 1932, he set out his policy idea of a New Deal. For the next three years a bewildering series of programmes, reforms and laws were passed to respond to what Roosevelt framed as a 'war against the emergency' following the Great Depression. This chain of activities, including agricultural and banking reform, work programmes, civil service wage and pension reforms and the end of prohibition, was labelled as part of a New Deal for the American public, and has since been labelled as a three-year-long New Deal part 1. This careful and consistent branding provided a rallying cry not only for its supporters, but also for its detractors, as Roosevelt acknowledged during one of his regular 'Fireside chat' radio broadcasts:

> A few timid people, who fear progress, will try to give you new and strange names for what we are doing. Sometimes they will call it 'Fascism', sometimes 'Communism', sometimes 'Regimentation', sometimes 'Socialism'. But, in so doing, they are trying to make very complex and theoretical something that is really very simple and very practical.
>
> (Roosevelt, 1934)

Roosevelt communicated his emerging definition of the New Deal – what it meant and what it didn't – through radio and public information films, and the American public wrote him letters expressing their views.

New Deal is a policy idea because it takes two words and joins them to create a unique compounded term, a vehicle by which to communicate a programme of public policy. Illustrated through a range of examples, this book explores how we attach a range of labels to these policy ideas that give them, at once, ideational, instrumental, visionary, container and brand-like characteristics. With the example of New Deal in mind, it is clear that policy ideas are by no means new as a mechanism. However, more thinking is needed to understand how such mechanisms operate in a modern communications environment.

Challenge 2: 'Surely there's nothing new under the sun, we just keep on recycling the same ideas over and over?'

When asked about policy ideas and where they come from, one of Robert Kingdon's respondents, quoted in his seminal text on Policy Agendas, replied that ideas are like perennials that lie dormant and then flower again (1995, p. 141). Another added that ideas are nothing new: 'We are resurrecting old dead dogs, sprucing them up, and then floating them up to the top' (1995, p. 173). For long-established public servants, 'new' policy initiatives seldom appear new. When prompted to discuss a new policy idea, they might well start with a story of how it was tried previously 20 years ago. But importantly, not all have this memory or make these associations: a colleague of those who make the 'dead dog' association may well view a scheme as something completely fresh and new, and attach a different set of subjective associations. This rather simplistic reasoning gives a glimmer of insight into how a 'new' idea can be both old and novel.

For some this prompts the question, 'where do ideas come from?' But asking such a question must also be paired with the question, 'how do ideas die?' In other words, what happens to all of the emotional attachment and sentiment directed at a policy idea that in many cases can occupy a central part of a civil servant's role for two or three years? So a core theme of this book is to explore not only what these policy ideas are, but how they are conceived and are born, how they live and, importantly, how they die.

Challenge 3: 'Surely the partial and shallow use of Twitter and Facebook offer just that: a partial and shallow discussion of policy issues?'

Benjamin Disraeli wrote of One Nation in 1845; Roosevelt of a New Deal in 1932; Harold MacMillan talked of a Middle Way in 1938; and Tony Blair of the Third Way in 1994. All these came before an era where people could publish their thoughts on a policy using a device in their pocket. David Cameron's Big Society from 2009 was introduced in press conferences and discussed on Twitter as #bigsociety (Cameron, 2009). As of June 2013, 487,000 tweets mentioning 'Big Society' and 47,000 mentioning '#bigsociety' had been published on the internet. Although the character limit on Twitter is less than 140 characters, to overlook what is happening within these data is short sighted.

Those sceptical of using social media data in policy analysis will commonly follow up with a question such as 'yes, but what proportion of the general public is active on Twitter?' When discussing public policy, the response needs to be a question back: 'what proportion of think tanks, columnists, politicians, senior civil servants, journalists, newspapers, media organisations, social scientists, bloggers, researchers, lobbyists and consultants are *not* on Twitter?' And of those not regularly tweeting or posting their views on other platforms, what proportion read tweets online or as quoted in their daily newspaper articles or mentioned by radio interviewers and TV presenters? In terms of those working on the frontline, what proportion of employers' organisations, unions, professional organisations and trade magazines do not have a Facebook page? What proportion of frontline NHS workers did not view the viral YouTube video attacking Andrew Lansley's NHS reforms or read some of the 2,500 comments below it (NxtGen & Gee, 2011)? Answers to questions of how policy is debated online remain somewhat unknown. This book joins the many other projects investigating the role of social media, bringing a particular focus on the 'social lives' of specific policy ideas.

Who this book is for

This book is aimed at academic researchers and postgraduate research students with an interest in policy analysis. Most readers will be drawn from the policy or political sciences; however, methods involved will be of interest to business analysts and psychologists. Although the author and many of the examples are based in the UK, the developments, methods and the concepts discussed are intended for an international audience. The contemporary and practice-focused subject matter means this book is likely to be of interest to policy practitioners and to the growing numbers of people interested in how to separate the signal from the noise in social media data, and the life and trajectory of ideas.

The methodological focus of the book will be familiar to those engaged with the interpretive policy analysis community and its associated annual conference. In particular, those interested in the principles underpinning political discourse theory will recognise this as an empirical application of this work. The focus on Q methodology will be of interest to the multi-disciplinary community of scholars and practitioners who use this method, particularly those interested in using Q in policy research and administering Q sorts online. The book is also relevant to social scientists interested in digital and text analytics, particularly the qualitative analysis of social media text and ways to overcome the challenges that arise in this type of work.

Although this is a research monograph rather than a text book per se, its focus on methods would be of interest to postgraduate research and doctoral training programmes.

Structure of the book

The book has eight chapters. Chapter 2 explores how policy ideas are conceptualised in different ways. It is based on five accounts or streams of literature. The first focuses on ideational accounts, ranging from Kingdon (1995) and his idea of perennial ideas, along with the political ideas (Braun & Busch, 1999; Gofas & Hay, 2012), to ideas in good currency (Schön, 1963), magic concepts (Pollitt & Hupe, 2011) and policy issues (Downs, 1972; Peters & Hogwood, 1985). It includes discussion of key symbols (Lasswell, 1949), labels (Edelman, 1977), keywords (Williams, 2013) and fuzzwords (Cornwall, 2007), and whether ideas are more akin to viruses, rather than products to be sold (Dudley & Richardson, 2001; Gofas, 2009; Richardson, 2000).

Importantly, Chapter 2 argues that there are four other accounts that require attention. First, the instrumental role of policy ideas as discourse (Schmidt, 2010), or ideas as roadmaps (Goldstein & Keohane, 1993) or purposive smokescreens (Reich, 1990). A second account focuses on the visionary qualities of policy ideas, like visions in urban planning (Shipley & Newkirk, 1999), the pursuit to coin a memorable phrase and the role of visions in energising and creating meaning and creative competition between narratives (Nanus, 1995). A third account focuses on the policy idea as a container concept that at its extension takes us into political philosophy, political discourse and empty signifiers (Laclau, 2005). Fourth, the policy idea as a brand – a slogan; as a compound (Benczes, 2006), but also as a brand that adds value, that is marketed, that diffuses, or perhaps follows the hype cycle of modern technologies. Illustrated through the case of the Big Society, the chapter argues that policy ideas can sustain all five kinds of label and have until now eluded definition.

Chapter 3 explores the lifecycle of policy ideas. It starts by considering the challenge of identifying the death and demise of policy ideas and, in doing so, revisits the policy science literature on policy termination. It sets out four models for measuring the life of a policy. The first is characterised as 'policy as activity', whereby a frequency graph measures fluctuation of discussion over time, as reflected in policy issues/policy cycles, newspaper citations and more recently search engine indexes, such as Google Trends (Choi & Varian, 2012). Although the 'policy as activity' metric predominates, this chapter discusses three alternative measures for the Y axis. For those interested in diffusion and growing market share, a 'policy as diffusion' model measures the maturity of the policy idea in terms of adoption of innovation, from early adopters to the late majority and laggards (Rogers, 2003). More recently, technology analytics are showing how it is preferable to measure 'policy as expectation', measuring the rising and falling 'hype' or expectation of user communities, as measured in hype cycles (Fenn & LeHong, 2011). Finally, the chapter proposes a model of 'policy as equivalence', whereby the policy idea is measured in terms of the process of actors attaching their demands to the policy idea, leading ultimately to dislocation. The 'policy as equivalence' model builds on earlier work (Jeffares, 2008) and is illustrated through the case of a policy idea called Flourishing Neighbourhoods, which was once popular in the English city of Birmingham.

Chapter 4 focuses in further detail on how the subjectivity surrounding a relatively new policy idea begins to crystallise into distinct viewpoints. The chapter introduces Q methodology (Brown, 1980; Stephenson, 1953), an approach increasingly used in policy analysis (Brewer et al., 2000; Cuppen, 2010; Durning, 1999; Jeffares & Skelcher, 2011). This involves first sampling the diversity of debate surrounding a policy idea in a set of statements of opinion, and presenting these to a diverse group of actors and asking them to rank order the statements and discuss their choices. By using a standard set of statements and instructions it is possible to correlate and factorise these sorts to identify shared viewpoints on the policy idea. This systematic process is designed to capture and find structure in what can often appear noisy or unstructured.

Chapter 4 explores how policy analysts are increasingly applying Q methodology and how they are currently sampling the concourse of debate surrounding policy ideas and related issues. The approach is illustrated through the case of the policy idea Total Place. The results reveal four distinct viewpoints at a point when the policy idea was in its relative infancy. However, importantly, the process also reveals the challenge of capturing a satisfactory volume of debate when the debate is taking place on so many different platforms, both on and off-line.

Chapter 5 reviews how policy practice is adapting to the availability of social media, and in particular, the micro-blogging platform Twitter. It illustrates how a range of policy actors might use the core functions of Twitter as part of their engagement with others. Such practices are illustrated through the case of the local PCC elections of November 2012.

Chapter 5 also reviews peer-reviewed literature, concluding that there are four imperatives driving social science research using Twitter and other social media data. It portrays a commercial imperative focused on 'return on investment' of social media campaigns, contrasted with a democratic imperative modelling uprising, contagion and open data. A political imperative led by psephologists seeks to understand politician use and predict election outcomes. Finally a fragmented set of literatures reflect a professional practice imperative in terms of how social media is changing the way that journalists, doctors, academics, civil servants, charities and law enforcers do their work. The review highlights how most resources are focused on commercial work, but often hidden behind opaque commercial sensitivities. Overall the chapter portrays a Gold rush for those seeking to unearth the secrets of what makes people take to the streets, vote for a candidate or buy a product. Policy-makers and the public services more generally have within their ranks early adopters, such as the police, who use social media to engage with and listen to their communities. Although some work explores policy-making in particular, there remain more questions than answers.

Chapter 6 focuses on the availability of social media data and how work is fragmenting into two camps characterised by their approach to data management: 'monitor and visualise' versus 'capture and sift'. The first draws on massive datasets owned and indexed by third party providers who charge for partial access to the data. While organisations might want to use this to monitor activity for the purposes of consumer insight or gathering intelligence, researchers are interested in the potential to historically track topics and identify critical moments, trends, fluctuations in sentiment or identify influential individuals. The alternative is to use software to capture and store social media data for the purposes of research. Researchers find themselves with several thousand/million items of data and related data about the data, known as metadata.

Chapter 6 applies both 'monitor and visualise' and 'capture and sift' approaches to the policy idea of PCCs, focusing particularly on engagement with content tagged with the Government's official policy campaign hashtag of '#MyPCC'. The chapter explores how the three week campaign prior to the PCC elections can be visualised, and key actors and themes revealed. It shows how samples of concourse can be taken daily for the purposes of tracking changing themes over time. It argues for the qualitative value of social media data and the limitations of automated sentiment meters.

Chapter 7 explores how policy actors use social media to express opinion about policy ideas. It considers methods to isolate social media activity that expresses opinion, repeats particular story-lines or applies critical tags. The chapter reports the process of crowdsourcing researchers to divide up coding tasks, each working on portions of the dataset in order to understand and organise a dataset. The chapter describes how the human coding informs Bayesian machine classifiers. It reports the thematic coding of PCC tweets and how this can then be used for a variety of purposes: it can inform how themes accumulate over time, how themes are spread across different data sources (such as Facebook, newspaper article comments and Twitter) and how thematic coding can be used to systematically generate samples for Q studies like that used in Chapter 4. In addition to the PCC election, two more policy ideas – Compassionate Care (in nursing/health reform) and the Bedroom Tax (in social housing/welfare reform) – are explored.

The book concludes by considering the implications for different readerships. For those in practice, key implications are that policy ideas are a core aspect of the policy landscape; that the apparent vagueness of an idea is part of its appeal; and that those who coin and foster ideas have to accept that organic labels will emerge. This chapter appeals to policy-makers to listen and engage through social media, while appreciating mortality and everyday subjectivity. For the growing number of social media analysts, this chapter calls for acknowledgement of emergent mediatised patterns of policy-making, and recommends resisting the temptation to reinvent standards and rules of social science. It is also important to share knowledge and approaches, and to acknowledge the value of single platforms and the value of qualitative analysis.

For policy analysis, this book concludes that specific policy programmes *are* indeed interesting, and may be understood by including the conversation beyond traditional sources. This will require policy analysis to develop and invest in new tools and techniques, embracing metrics beyond frequency and major disruptive events and focusing on everyday subjectivity. Importantly in this area, policy analysis need not be divided by choice of data source; social media data is a common treasury for all types of analysis, from quantitative models to ethnography.

2
Theorising Policy Ideas

What is a policy idea? In 2009, the soon-to-be Conservative Prime Minister David Cameron set out an idea where the people of Britain worked out answers to big social problems, saying that 'A big part of that answer is the Big Society. I think we are on to a really big idea' (Cameron, 2009). Once elected into government, Cameron continued, for the first year or two at least, to set out his vision for a Big Society. The idea attracted international attention, as far afield as Australia (Whelan et al., 2012). It led many scholars to interrogate the intention and charter of this type of policy-making by big idea (Alcock, 2010; Bailey & Pill, 2011; Cotterill et al., 2012; Davies & Pill, 2012; Evans, 2011; Glasman & Norman, 2012; Kettell, 2012; Mycock & Tonge, 2011; Pattie & Johnston, 2011; Sullivan, 2012). Previous work has been largely concerned with the meaning of policy ideas like the Big Society; this chapter instead asks what these big ideas are, and explores the issues prompted by asking such a question.

This chapter responds to a contradiction. It seeks to explore how policy ideas like the Big Society can be simultaneously defined: ideationally as 'big ideas' or part of a 'broader ideology'; instrumentally as 'programmes', or 'smokescreens'; as 'genuine visions', or 'grotesque fantasies'; as containing 'empty rhetoric' or 'without definition'; as 'party brands' or 'soundbites'.

This chapter asks: what do we mean by policy idea? The term evokes a variety of images and synonyms drawn from a range of literatures across academia. This chapter seeks to acknowledge the many synonyms for policy idea and arrive at a definition of what a policy idea is and what a policy idea is not.

Intuitively, policy ideas are an essential element of governing. Policy ideas are crisp, terse, evocative, current, carefully chosen compounds of two familiar words: *Big Society, Troubled Families, Forward Guidance*. This chapter argues that the implementation and influence of public policy includes the coining and fostering of policy ideas to frame problems, solutions or idealised futures (Edelman, 1977). Although some policy ideas outlast their makers, it seems most last weeks and months rather than years and decades.

The rise and fall of policy ideas and agendas has long been a fascination of academia (Downs, 1972). Policy ideas need to be understood as much for their ideational qualities as their visionary, brand-like, instrumental and absorptive qualities. Understanding policy ideas requires us to draw on a broad range of literatures and disciplines including lexicography, computing, marketing and political philosophy.

Indeed, the Big Society was launched as a policy idea celebrating the contribution of organisations and individuals beyond the state. It embraced popular principles of social capital and community empowerment. Introduced during the election campaign as a set of principles rather than specific promises, one advocate argued during a Commons debate:

> The Big Society is the most important idea in British politics for a generation ... a fundamental rethinking that tries to lay the groundwork for our social and economic renewal as a nation. As such, its natural span is not over days and weeks, but years and perhaps decades.
> (Jesse Norman, in Hansard, 2011)

Despite a lack of detail, it created a considerable stir among think tanks, bloggers, local government and the voluntary sector. The lack of substance also attracted considerable scorn, with critics taking the opportunity to claim that the Big Society was 'a cover for "big cuts"', or an ideological reaction to big government. Key people were announced as leading the Big Society idea, notably Lord Wei, a management consultant and community organiser, and Steve Hilton, Cameron's then Director of Strategy. Shortly after the 2010 General Election, further detail was added, including ideas for a Big Society bank. By early 2011 the press and academic criticism was mounting. A speech on the Big Society in June 2011 was labelled by the media as the third 'relaunch'. Newspaper articles, comments on Twitter and parliamentary debate included arguments that the Big Society was a 'dead parrot', a 'busted flush', 'Cameron's millennium dome'. They argued that it was too vague, too meaningless, a policy idea that nobody could define or understand.

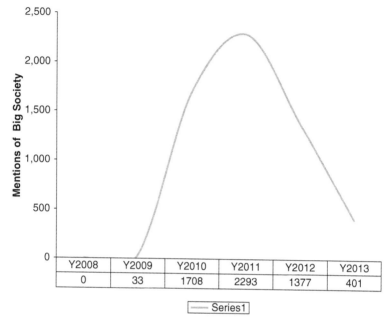

	Y2008	Y2009	Y2010	Y2011	Y2012	Y2013
	0	33	1708	2293	1377	401

Series1

Figure 2.1   Mentions of 'Big Society' in UK broadsheet newspapers
Source: Nexis UK.

Indeed, tracking newspaper citations in UK broadsheets, Figure 2.1 shows that articles mentioning the Big Society peaked in 2011 with 2293 articles, reducing to 1377 in 2012 and just 401 in 2013.

The drop-off in mentions follows the assertion that the Big Society is a policy idea in decline, possibly dying. How much we should read into this is discussed in later chapters. Before it is possible to understand the lifecycle of policy ideas it is important to set out with greater precision our conceptual understanding of policy ideas. It seems appropriate to start with ideational conceptions: the policy idea as a form of political idea.

Policy ideas as ideas

When political scientists write about the role or importance of political ideas (Blyth, 1997, 2002, 2013; Braun & Busch, 1999; Campbell, 2002; Finlayson, 2004; Gofas & Hay, 2012; Hay & Wincott, 1998; Schmidt & Radaelli, 2004) their unit of analysis typically ranges from the macro, such as worldview ideologies (e.g. libertarianism) to something at the 'middle range' exemplified by Berman (2009), and occasionally the micro, referring to specific policy initiatives. Acknowledging how most focus on the macro ideas (Hall, 1989; Hay & Wincott, 1998), Berman argues for her preference for what she calls 'middle range', as for her, 'world views are...too broad to be useful', whereas policy positions 'may be too narrow to be interesting' (Berman, 2009, p. 21). Political ideas might be attributed to a particular actor, place or time, but in the main they have no 'owner'. Micro-level political ideas on the contrary do have an identifiable owner or inventor who first named and launched the initiative, policy or programme. This chapter, and indeed this book, frames Berman's assertion as something of a challenge. Yes, as ideas they are narrow; but they are by no means uninteresting. To overlook them in our analysis is to neglect an important aspect of the study of public policy. This book is therefore written in defence of specific, narrow, named political initiatives as worthy of study.

Although ideationalists distinguish between levels or types of ideas, when it comes to understanding how and why ideas come to be adopted or become fashionable, the nuances are lost. Across the social sciences, 'ideas' are expressed in numerous ways, as concepts that are in vogue, fashionable, have 'caught on', or 'ideas in good currency' (Schön, 1963). For instance, Lasuen spoke of catchwords as ideas in good currency that enjoy a mythical status, and that also enjoy the dual status of being both useful and yet loosely defined. He argues that this special class of ideas eventually 'pass away, undestroyed', in that blame is placed on the inefficiency of those implementing the idea rather than the idea itself (1969, p. 139). As discussed in Chapter 1, ideas are argued to be rarely new; rather, they are akin to perennials that lie dormant and flower again, or resurrections of 'old dead dogs' (Kingdon, 1995, p. 173).

In public management literatures, ideas such as 'innovation' are conceptualised as magic concepts that come to dominate for period of time (Pollitt & Hupe, 2011): policy issues such as 'economic policy' or 'international affairs' are argued to rise and fall in cyclical patterns (Downs, 1972; Hogwood & Peters, 1982; Peters & Hogwood, 1985). For Lasswell, such ideas were key symbols – basic terms such as 'freedom', 'democracy' and 'equality' that are 'common experience for everyone in the state, ranging from the most powerful boss to the humblest layman or philosopher' – it is about everybody having 'exposure to the same set of key words' (Lasswell, 1949, p. 13).

There are a myriad of other labels of ideas that highlight broad themes about what such ideas are. Ideas are labels for social problems, mythical populations, enemies, segments and crises (Edelman, 1977). Ideas, like the Big Society, are keywords that gain popularity in popular and academic discourse (Bennett et al., 2005; Williams, 2013). Ideas are buzzwords that are popular within particular disciplines and sections of society, but are also 'fuzzwords' with a capacity to cloud understanding (Cornwall & Eade, 2010).

Distinctions are made between ideas as saleable products and free-floating virus-like entities (Gofas, 2009) that can cause epidemics (Gladwell, 2006) or memes that spread (Chesterman, 1997). Richardson argues that ideas as viruses have the ability to 'disrupt existing policy systems, power relationships and policies', with policy communities confronted with the choice of either attempting to adapt the virus, or mutating themselves (2000, p. 1018).

If ideas in policy and organisational literatures are cast as catchwords, magic concepts, keywords, key symbols, buzzwords and viruses, to what extent is this visible in press and parliamentary discourse surrounding the Big Society? Below I consider a Nexis UK search of 1,009 UK national newspaper articles mentioning 'Big Society' between December 2010 and March 2011. I contrast this with a transcript of a five hour Commons debate on the Big Society held on 28 February 2011 (Hansard, 2011). The debate includes contributions from all political parties, resulting in a transcript of 50,000 words. Although by no means exhaustive, the archive is sufficiently comprehensive to give a flavour of how a policy idea such as the Big Society is conceptualised by journalists and politicians during its peak (Figure 2.1).

Analysis of the press and parliamentary archive shows that 'idea' is by far the most common descriptor for the Big Society: as well as describing the Big Society as 'a policy idea' it is framed as 'an exciting idea', an 'important idea', a 'neutral idea', a 'novel idea'. For others the Big Society is 'an idea as old as the hills', 'a doomed idea', or 'an idea, but not new'. Other appeals to ideas place the Big Society as part of a 'governing philosophy', 'a belief', or 'a mentality'. We find claims that the Big Society is neither a 'left or right wing idea' (Jesse Norman MP), that it is not left, right or centre (Albert Own MP). Some argue that the Big Society idea is novel in how it recognises both people and institutions (Chris White MP), whereas others refute claims that this is new: that 'passing power from state to citizen and encouraging people to be empowered in their own communities is an idea as old as the hills' (Steve Brine); that the Big Society is an idea that is 'neither new nor free' (Nic Dakin MP).

These accounts of the Big Society correspond with common ideationalist accounts in terms of ideas in common currency, the mutation of a viral idea or a resurrection of old ideas, but framing the Big Society as an idea also presents us with a problem of scale. While some claim that the Big Society is more than a mere initiative, arguing that it is the expression of a deeper ideology, it places the Big Society as akin to a catchword or keyword, like 'democracy' or 'equality'. Framing the Big Society as an idea downplays the specificity, particularity, the self-conscious development of the Big Society. Contained within both the Hansard transcript and newspaper archive are alternative conceptions. Four other kinds of conception are visible, outlined below.

First, for some, the Big Society was conceptualised specifically as a policy *instrument,* like this example from Hunt, labelling it as a 'vehicle':

> The Big Society is being used as a vehicle for justifying some of the major cuts and assaults on the state that we are seeing today.
>
> (Tristram Hunt MP)

In other instances it was conceptualised as an aspiration, something closer to a normative or idealised *vision,* as in this example from Chris Heaton-Harris, in which he personifies the Big Society as being embodied by one of his constituents:

> Those who work the hardest in society, and who have the least net disposable income, the 'squeezed middle', are the ones who go out of their way to give time to and help their communities. Those people are the Big Society... In my constituency, it is dead simple. The Big Society is a lady called Fiona Tompkinson.
>
> (Chris Heaton-Harris MP)

In other instances the lack of a particular definition was the defining characteristic of the Big Society in terms of its capacity to *contain,* or be attached to, a broad range of projects and definitions, expressed in this example by Mark Williams in terms of bafflement:

> I suspect that by the time [the debate] ends, at 10 pm, we shall have been given 30 definitions of what the Big Society is. People are increasingly familiar with the phrase, but they are still some-what baffled about what it means. We have a chance to address that this afternoon. The concept is not well defined and neither is it understood yet.
>
> (Mark Williams MP)

A final and somewhat commonplace conceptualisation of the Big Society was as a product to be *branded* and sold, expressed here by Hoise, arguing that the Big Society is a

> Rebranding of what already happens the length and breadth of the country.
>
> (Stewart Hoise MP)

These examples serve to illustrate how a policy idea like the Big Society can be simultaneously conceptualised as an idea, an instrument of power, a vision for the future, a point of coherence and a brand being sold. This diversity of descriptors leads us beyond a narrow reading of ideational literatures to consider a broader conceptual consideration of what these policy ideas are. The chapter now turns to explore these alternative conceptions in greater detail, starting with an instrumental view of policy ideas.

The instrument

The Big Society archive repeatedly frames the policy as an instrument of governing, a key aspect of a wider change agenda. Rather than ideational descriptors, the Big Society is labelled as a 'manifesto' or 'flagship policy', an 'initiative', something to be 'launched', a 'plan', a 'programme', a 'project', a 'scheme', a 'set of proposals', a 'claim'.

This instrumental conception of the Big Society policy idea attributes ownership, particularly to the British prime minister himself, with examples of the Big Society as 'Cameron's policy idea' or 'Cameron's mission in politics'. In a similar vein, the Big Society is positioned as one element of a broader idea, such as the outcome of decentralisation, or part of a 'laissez-faire regime', or an agenda for a smaller state. One common instrumental claim from Labour MPs was that the Big Society was somehow being used as a mask or a smokescreen, covering over alternative agendas. Here we find a variety of descriptors including the Big Society as 'a cloak', a 'big con', 'bull shit', 'cuddly spin', a 'spin on privatisation', a 'smokescreen for massive cuts', a 'cover for cuts', or a 'vehicle carrying cuts'. This argument is consistent across several newspapers.

In an editorial bearing the headline 'Big Society is a big con', it was argued that, 'Blow away the Big Society smokescreen and all that remains is a Tory Government dedicated to cutting services and raising taxes' (Mirror, 2011, p. 8). Similarly *The Times* reported a poll that 78% of the British public thought 'The Big Society is just an attempt by government to put a positive spin on the damage public spending cuts are doing to local communities' (Times, 2011, p. 2). Similar arguments are evident in the parliamentary debate:

> We fear that much of this talk of the Big Society is an ideologically driven smokescreen for large-scale Government cuts.
>
> (Susan Elan Jones MP)

> I resist the simple notion that the Big Society is a sham and simply a veneer for ideologically driven cuts.
>
> (Jon Cruddas MP)

> If the Big Society is not just rhetorical cover for cuts in public services, the Prime Minister must demonstrate through actions rather than words.
>
> (Nic Dakin MP)

This instrumental view of policy ideas leads us away from conceptions of ideas catching on, to the instrumental role of discourse (Schmidt & Radaelli, 2004). It also leads us away from rationalist accounts that ideas serve to enable rational actors to realise their interests, and the role of ideas is to serve as roadmaps, guiding actors towards their preferences (Goldstein & Keohane, 1993). The instrumental account of policy ideas focuses our attention on what Moore would call 'self-consciously developed and promoted ideas' attempting to 'produce significant effects on public policy' (Moore, 1990, p. 80). Yet Moore also reminds us in the same breath that 'it is almost certain that they cannot be produced singlehandedly by an individual without reference to the institutional context' (Moore, 1990).

However tempting it might be to argue that policy ideas are mere instruments of power, the cynical invention of despotic and self-servingly rational leaders, the question of popular appeal goes unanswered. To understand the popular appeal of a policy idea, as Reich argues, we need to move beyond arguments that policy ideas are mere smokescreens for institutions (1990).

The vision

Part of the popular appeal of the Big Society as a policy idea is how it projects a particular vision of the future. Several descriptors for the Big Society invoke its 'visionary' qualities: 'a vision for Britain', a 'vision for society', 'a genuine vision', 'a Big Society dream', 'a grotesque fantasy'.

The Big Society was also described as an imagined community, for 'people that help their community', 'groups meeting in village halls', and 'underlying communities'. Those that embrace the Big Society are labelled as 'ambassadors' and 'trailblazers'. These are communities, subsets of society said to exist outside government and its reach. This type of descriptor is used to define the Big Society as something that is already operating in some neighbourhoods, especially places that live on despite economic hardship; it is a vision embodied by people who help their communities.

A visionary conception of the Big Society can be found in several of the parliamentary extracts, for example:

> Many politicos who are sceptical about the Big Society ask, 'What does it mean? What does it stand for?' They want that all-important buzzword to describe it, but they should take it from someone who has spent their working life in it: the Big Society is so big that no word could possibly do it justice.
>
> (Stuart Andrew MP)

> Big Society is a wonderful thing. To those philosophers who say that this bird cannot fly, I say that it does fly. They should come to Cumbria ... It is about communities and community action.
>
> (Rory Stewart MP)

> To me, the Big Society is about the message that we missed in the '50s and '60s with the great slum clearances and again in the '80s and '90s with regeneration. That is the fact that however bad an area seems from the outside, it still possesses something of the Big Society and there is some community there, however bare it is.
>
> (Eric Ollerenshaw MP)

> I met another disabled access group ... meeting almost every week for more than 10 years to improve their lives by discussing ideas and common issues ... I contend that the Big Society is out there and is operating.
>
> (Henry Smith)

In business and urban planning literatures alike, visions are important to describe a desirable situation in a future time (Hopkins & Zapata, 2007; Shipley, 2000; Shipley & Newkirk, 1999). In the 1980s it became popular for cities to develop and publicise long term visions for the future, often as part of a strategic regeneration or marketing strategy

(Shipley, 2000). These visions were commonly expressed through the use of a memorable phrase or label. Visions were prized for helping to make long term projects a success (Christenson & Walker, 2008). This interest in the power of visions spawned a literature around how to create successful visions for the future (Allen, 1995). For van Hulst and Gerrits, visions are simplified mental accounts. The act of visioning stems from a desire of humans to make complexity manageable by creating simplified images through slogans, logos, rhetorical statements and simplified stories (van Hulst & Gerrits, 2008). 'This simplification helps in two ways: it creates an understandable reality for them to work in and it offers an understandable relation for others to adhere to' (van Hulst & Gerrits, 2008, p. 4).

Van Hulst and Gerrits suggest that if the vision for the future is too concrete or idealised it can fail to unite actors, aid decision-making or improve understanding. The authors propose that visioning should allow for a type of storytelling in which actors construct, deconstruct and reconstruct collective identities in what are changing actor constellations. They say 'the goal is not to define a clear future but to establish a process of creative competition between narratives' (van Hulst & Gerrits, 2008, p. 16).

On this basis, we can say that the method by which the Big Society was announced allowed for multiple definitions to flourish. It allowed space for critique and strong criticism that, paradoxically, might well have contributed to its longer term appeal. The quotes from Hansard above show this neatly; each MP has a particular image of the Big Society in mind. While this led to accusations that the idea was nebulous and vague, following van Hulst and Gerrits, it also allowed space for creative competition between alternative narratives.

The container

A frequently discussed characteristic of policy ideas is that they evade definition. For example, descriptors of the Big Society include charges of it being 'empty rhetoric', an 'empty gesture', meaning 'everything and nothing', an 'abstract concept', 'abstract notion', 'the idea no one understands', a 'vague idea', a concept that 'is not well defined'. This lack of clear definition is expressed in the following Hansard extracts:

> I am still struggling to understand what the Big Society is and nobody sitting on the Benches opposite has really explained it to me. We can

all give examples of what we think it is and what we think it should do, but we have never heard a definition.

(Albert Owen)

One of the 300 questions that I have tabled on the issue of the 'Big Society' asks the Minister to define what it is. The answer has come back, and I have been told that there is no definition.

(Chris Ruane)

Similarly, by 2011, journalists and commentators began to highlight how 'conventional wisdom [is] gather[ing] around the idea that no one understands what the Big Society is supposed to be' (Carr, 2011), and argue that in terms of launching and 'promoting a rather vague idea, David Cameron is in a class of his own' (Gimson, 2011, p. 10). In response to a *Guardian* article entitled 'Big Society is a busted flush', Sarah Lesniewksi questions why so many organisations have invested resources in what she argues is an 'empty gesture':

Whether out of naivety or self-interest (the more likely case), organisations have spent the nine months since the election intently focused on dissecting, discussing, and poring over this empty gesture, instead of speaking out against its obvious fallacies, strategising, and taking decisive action against the regressive policies and cuts which are now bringing down the communities they claim to represent.

(Lesniewksi, 2011, p. 31)

In the wider literature, this charge that ideas are often empty, vague or meaningless is a familiar one and expands on van Hulst and Gerrits's point about fostering visions that are vague enough to unite actors. The balance between steering a policy idea between the accommodating and the meaningless is a difficult balance to strike, but it seems that the most efficacious policy ideas function as containers into which demands, agendas, meanings and definitions can be accommodated. This has led to policy ideas being labelled by some as 'container concepts' (Baker, 2008, p. 250). The garbage can thesis of Cohen et al. 1972 describes this process by which policy is made by throwing agendas into an empty vessel. The very appeal of the policy idea is its unfinished, ill-defined nature, as this appears to offer opportunities to contribute and influence. At the same time, for some, the way in which meaning around policy often fragments can help to explain why policies fail (Fotaki, 2010).

The literature conceptualises a scenario in which a policy idea can achieve a precarious status, where it lacks precise definition yet is loaded with demands. This status is described by political discourse theorists as the status of the empty signifier. Inspired by the work of Laclau and Mouffe (Griggs & Howarth, 2011; Howarth et al., 2000; Howarth, 2000; Howarth & Torfing, 2005; Laclau & Mouffe, 2001; Torfing, 1999, 2005), these theorists see the political sphere as being made up of policy actors articulating 'demands' which have a habit of chaining together in opposition to a common enemy. When applied to social movements, it explains the unlikely alliance between 'Volvos and vegans' in the proposals for a second runway at Manchester Airport (Griggs & Howarth, 2008).

The empty signifier symbolises that which is missing from this set of demands, and symbolises an absent fullness yet to come. The empty signifier originates from the chain of the demands; it is both an ordinary demand and has a special status as the 'general equivalent' for the whole chain (Laclau, 2005). Once established as a 'discourse', further demands are added. As the chain grows longer, the capacity for the empty signifier to represent the whole chain is challenged (Torfing, 1999).

Through this lens, Cameron's policy idea of the Big Society, at its peak in 2011, was an empty signifier that can be conceptualised as attempting to hold together a precarious range of demands, both his own principles for reform and that of his party and Coalition partners: Like the container concept and garbage can thesis, as an empty signifier the Big Society has the capacity to hold together a broad range of demands. Contrary to Sarah Lesniewksi's point above – that actors are investing in the Big Society idea out of self-interest – the Big Society as empty signifier casts actors as engaged in the pursuit of completeness rather than self-interest. This pursuit of completeness sees policy actors striving for the achievement of an unthreatened and fully fledged identity. They are seeking the impossible idea of 'closure and fullness' (Howarth et al., 2000, p. 8). So when people associate with the Big Society they are investing their demands. They are subscribers seeking completeness.

The Big Society, drawn as an empty signifier, goes some way to describing how policy actors seek to attach demands to high profile yet vague policy ideas. But as self-consciously created ideas, the original sponsors, that is, the creators of these policy ideas, have specific aims or intentions for their idea. They have an idea to sell and a message to manage.

The brand

A fifth and final conceptualisation of policy ideas like the Big Society places emphasis on their role as brands. In the archive, the Big Society is variably described as 'a brand', 'a concept', as 'party branding', a 'phrase', a 'catchy phrase', a 'slogan', an 'official slogan', 'rhetoric', a 'sound-bite' and a 'sign'.

Politicians argue that the Big Society is part of a

> ...Rebranding of the Conservative party by an excellent public relations manager.
>
> (Nic Dakin)

> 'Big Community' would have been a better idea and concept to sell.
>
> (Albert Owen)

In the literature, policy ideas are viewed as slogans, defined by Lasswell as 'a terse string of words that gain meaning by repetition and context' (Lasswell, 1949, p. 13).

Lexicographically, the Big Society is a neologism, or a new word. Algeo suggests that more than two-thirds of new words are based on combining existing words, or morphemes, most of which are compounds, that is 'two (occasionally more) words combined in a lexical unit. They are usually written with a space between them... less often solid... or written with a hyphen' (Algeo, 1993, p. 7). Lexicographers concerned with trends in new words have noted a general acceleration in their appearance, and the emergence of verb-headed compounds, such as *trail blaze* or *stir fry* (Bagasheva, 2011). That is not to say that all policy ideas are verb-headed, but it offers some suggestion of the kinds of terms that can be combined by policy actors.

The motivation for new words is pragmatic. It is about naming 'new things' or talking about 'old things in a new way'. This, it is argued, is driven by material and intellectual change, where 'invention, discovery, exploration, war, commerce and revolution all breed neology' (Algeo, 1993, p. 14). As neology, coining a policy idea is the act of 'creative compounding' (Benczes, 2006) where existing words, like 'big' and 'society' are combined to coin a unique and brand-like term. For policy actors, a key aspect of the task of defining a new problem to be tackled or outlining a programme of reform includes the ability to coin a suitably unique neologism. It is a task of inventing a new term for the policy problem or the policy solution. To succeed at policy-making is to be able to creatively compound, to coin new terms, to name new policy ideas.

Creating a unique name for policy ideas allows them to be branded. The Big Society as a brand becomes something to be created, marketed and protected, something to promote as memorable and credible. The literature argues that branding offers a wealth of benefits in policy-making. It aids agenda setting, provides boundaries for focusing and directing behaviour. It aids implementation by getting policies accepted and helps to foster positive associations by symbolising strength (Eshuis & Edwards, 2012, pp. 6–7). A brand, they argue, serves as 'a symbolic construct meant to add value to a product. It is not the product itself but [the branding that] gives meaning and value to the product, and defines its identity' (Eshuis & Edwards, 2012, p. 3).

Conclusion

This chapter has explored five alternative conceptualisations of policy ideas, drawing on a variety of literatures and illustrated through journalistic and parliamentary discussion of the 'Big Society'. The chapter explored ideational conceptions of political ideas 'whose time has come', and beyond to consider them instruments of power; as symbolising an idealised vision; or as accommodating a broad range of demands and agendas. The discussion concluded by focusing on policy ideas as the result of creative compounding – the creation of a new unique term that can be branded as something with hard identity and yet with soft definition; a brand ready to be marketed by a small group of protagonists.

Although the five conceptions bring us closer to a definition of policy ideas, it also prompts us to further understand how such policy ideas live and die. The chapter began with the depiction in Figure 2.1 of how the Big Society had peaked around 2011 in terms of newspaper citations, and therefore substantiating the argument of some commentators that the idea was dead, as this quote colourfully argues:

> The Big Society theme is now, in effect, dead – its corpse riddled with bullets fired by a jealous government machine that had no intention of relinquishing any power.
>
> (Gimson, 2011)

Arguing that a policy is dead is part and parcel of politics, but it does raise interesting questions. This chapter focused on making explicit the varied means by which we conceptualise policy ideas; the next chapter takes up the challenge of understanding more about their lifecycle: how policy ideas are conceived, born, live and die.

3
The Lifecycle of Policy Ideas

Policy actors have long been known to attempt to coin and foster policy ideas and yet ambiguity remains in our understanding of their emergence and life expectancy. This chapter explores the lifecycle of policy ideas, from their origins to their demise.

Flourishing Neighbourhoods was a policy idea popular in Birmingham between 2001 and 2003. Throughout the 1980s it was widely reported that city leaders had pursued a Detroit-style investment in five-star hotels, business tourism and shopping centres as part of an urban renaissance. The introduction of the Flourishing Neighbourhoods policy in 2001, it was argued, was an attempt to transfer the success of the city centre renaissance to its wider suburbs, which still numbered among the poorest in the country.

Flourishing Neighbourhoods had a thousand day lifecycle (Jeffares, 2008). It ceased to be mentioned in the press with any volume after the election of a new administration in 2004. There was, however, no formal acknowledgement or death notice that Flourishing Neighbourhoods had been terminated. It was documented as something scrapped by the former council leader:

> Sir Albert Bore, former council boss and leader of the Labour group [asked] why ... had the [new] coalition scrapped the appellation flourishing neighbourhoods when referring to the Birmingham suburbs in favour of vibrant urban villages?
>
> (Birmingham Post, 2004)

Both this quote and Gimson's depiction in the last chapter of the Big Society as riddled with bullets remind us that visionary and purposeful policy ideas are mortal and have a limited lifespan, but certifying this death is somewhat subjective. It is an act of politics.

The difficulty of certifying the death of a policy initiative provokes a revisit of the literature on policy termination (DeLeon, 1977; Ferry & Bachtler, 2013). In the mid-1970s this work originated to address the question of what follows the linear policy process of formulation-initiation-implementation-termination. Policy termination scholars are the pathologists of the policy sciences, asking questions as to how, when and why a policy dies. These policy pathologists report that policy ideas are vulnerable from their very inception; 'most policies will already have generated their own congeries of critics that can be expected to coalesce behind the termination proposal' (DeLeon, 1977, pp. 283–284). Unlike organisations, policy ideas cannot build alliances, they have to prove their worth and cannot be 'hardwired', but rather have to adapt to survive (Boin et al., 2010). Yet it also seems impossibly difficult to certify their demise, as is evident in the policy termination literature that tends to focus on the demise of tangible artefacts such as organisations, rather than policy initiatives per se.

As Parsons puts it:

> Problems are born, policies grow up, and then wither and die. However, although policy genesis is easy enough to identify the moment of policy death is less certifiable.
>
> (Parsons, 1995, p. 574)

How this literature frames the termination of policy is, nevertheless, a useful starting point. Consider for example their dependent variables – the idea of lifespan, and how they define termination as abolition, merger or split (Boin et al., 2010). Consider also the questions they pose: '*Why some public organisations die whereas others persist?*' (Boin et al., 2010). They consider possible causes or independent variables to explain this variation in life expectancy, such as the arrival of new governments, ideological de-legitimation, turbulence, sunset clauses, functional redundancy, environmental changes or particular birth characteristics (Bardach, 1976; Parsons, 1995).

If faced with the cases of the Big Society or Flourishing Neighbourhoods, it can be imagined that these policy termination pathologists would set about comparing the lifecyle of policy ideas in terms of what form the termination took (was it abolition, merger or split?) and which internal characteristics, such as particular 'birth defects' (Boin et al., 2010), might have contributed to its demise.

However, rather than take such a policy pathologist approach and seek to objectify the death of what are inherently political policy ideas, a better starting point is revealed by asking the simple question, 'is this policy idea dead?' Asking this question brings into focus the practice of policy actors of conceiving, naming and fostering policy ideas, with their births announced and celebrated across multiple platforms. It brings into focus how policy communities invest time and resources in implementing or seeking to influence the direction or meaning of policy ideas. It brings into focus the mortality of particular policy ideas, time limited to a lifecycle of a few months or years. Asking such a question reveals how historic policy ideas can be easily forgotten, displaced by a positive story of the latest and loudest; a principle illustrated by Sir James George Frazer's observation of Saharan Tuaregs in the 1920s:

> They dread the return of the dead man's spirit, and do all they can to avoid it by shifting their camp after death, ceasing to ever pronounce the name of the departed and eschewing everything that might be regarded as an evocation or recall of his soul...they never speak of So-and-So, son of So-and-So; they give every man a name which will live and die with him.
>
> (Frazer, 2009, p. 259)

In his infamous article, '12 hints for how to terminate a public policy', Robert Behn suggests: 'Adoption, Not Termination. Political Leaders do not like to terminate policies' (Behn, 1978, p. 408). Drawing on the work of Peter deLeon, Behn argues that political leaders seek to avoid negative connotations of policy termination, preferring to focus on initiating 'new and better policies...termination of policy A may be best realised though the adoption of policy B'. Behn describes this as 'obfuscating the termination', privileging political expedience at the expense of long-term implementation. Unlike the loss of an organisation, the termination of a policy can easily fall below the radar, which links to a further reason for the lack of research in this area: methodological difficulty.

Parsons is right to argue that certifying the death of policies requires 'a very sensitive device to measure their demise and final extinction' (1995). Although scholars such as Boin and colleagues demonstrate methodological rigour in how they explore the various causes of termination, Greenwood raises the challenge of differentiating between function, policy and programme, or, for that matter, how to deal with whether something is a termination or a succession (Greenwood, 1997).

This challenge is something of a methodological one: how to track a policy over time. Unlike tracking broader political ideas, the brand-like uniqueness of a policy idea makes tracking and quantifying seem plausible. Figure 2.1 in the previous chapter, did just that, counting the frequency of citations of the Big Society in broadsheet newspapers. The following section explores the possibilities and limitations of tracing policies over time and frames these approaches in terms of measuring activity, diffusion and expectation.

Tracking policy activity, diffusion and expectation

This section explores three approaches to tracking a policy idea over time, starting with a measure of activity. Over the years many writers have taken the lead from Downs and his issue attention cycle (Downs, 1972). Peters and Hogwood explore how broader policy issues rise and fall in cyclical fashion over time (Peters & Hogwood, 1985). With a policy initiative the task is more concrete. Writing back in the mid-1990s, Parsons suggested the possibility of tracking a policy initiative by plotting the number of newspaper articles. Gone are the days of microfiche and newspaper indexes; tools such as Nexis UK (formerly LexisNexis) offer researchers the opportunity to search for articles mentioning a specific policy initiative and amass an electronic corpus of text (e.g., Grundmann & Krishnamurthy, 2010).

More recently the arrival of Google Trends allows us to visualise the frequency of terms entered into online search engines (see Figure 3.1). While its high profile use has shown the ability to reflect, and even predict, the spread of the flu virus across the US, it can also be applied to the more high profile policy ideas (Choi & Varian, 2012).

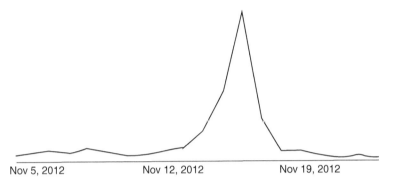

| Nov 5, 2012 | Nov 12, 2012 | Nov 19, 2012 |

Figure 3.1   Search activity for the term 'PCC' November 2012
Source: Google Trends.

What these approaches share is an X axis of time and a Y axis of activity. This *policy as activity* model prompts us to think of the rise and fall of rival agendas. It makes it possible to plot one policy against another and tempts us into drawing conclusions. Where it is at its most useful is in how it gives us insight into the very first use of a policy idea – its first public exposure to the press, or web searches. When several policy ideas are compared in one chart they depict the daily fluctuating activity of policy ideas as something akin to carousel horses rising and falling in cyclical motion.

In terms of tracking policy by activity, their fluctuation according to frequency of use is only one metric. An alternative metric for the Y axis is to focus on diffusion in terms of adoption or awareness. One of the longest established metrics for measuring policy over time can be drawn from the innovation literature. This work stems from the influential work of (Rogers, 2003) and colleagues. 'Uptake' is depicted on the Y axis in Figure 3.2, and the graphic plots the diffusion of the entity over time. The resulting 'S curve' has been widely applied, from uptake of products to awareness of major incidents. This temporal plotting also focuses on when and who adopts the object of study, which leads to the discussion of the roles of 'opinion leaders', 'change agents', the role of mass media and influence of interpersonal communication. It also defines those

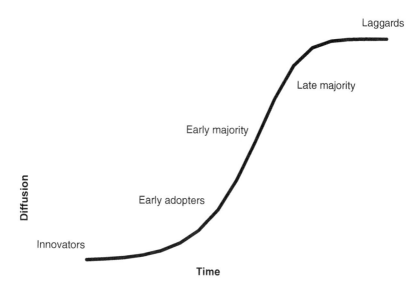

Figure 3.2   Policy as diffusion: a stylized model of diffusion

adopting the object by when they accepted it, colourfully labelling them as innovators, early adopters, members of the late majority or laggards.

This approach tracks the policy idea in terms of actor awareness or engagement. This lens helps us to see that early adopters of the discussion are often closely connected to political elites – perhaps academics, agents in consultancies or think tanks (Stone, 1999). Here we can find discussion of the policy issues taking place in workshops or meetings, in specialist publications or blog posts, several months before the issue is reported by newspapers or enters the consciousness of frontline workers or service users. Such a framing of 'policy as diffusion' is reflected in Cornford's remark that think tanks are like performing fleas, hopping around and stinging the body politic (Cornford, 1990). What is compelling about this analogy is the idea that early adopters engage with policy ideas at the early stages of their formulation, perhaps as contractors or at least commentators and discussants. At the point where the policy idea is mainstream, they intuitively 'hop off', turning their attention to the next big policy idea.

A third alternative to 'policy as activity' or 'policy as diffusion' is found in hype cycle analytics (Fenn & LeHong, 2011), where the Y axis now measures expectation rather than frequency, adoption or exposure: this is 'policy as expectation'. The hype cycle, depicted in Figure 3.3, was developed mainly for tracking the journey of technologies, either

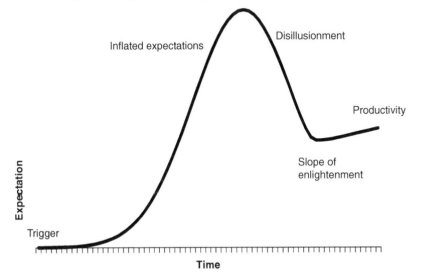

Figure 3.3   Policy as expectation: a stylized model of a hype cycle

specific products or emergent technologies such as Wi-Fi, VoIP or iPods. The pattern they observe, and, it is argued, that most technologies share, is a twin peaked trajectory.

The hype cycle is sub-divided into five stages: the technology trigger, the peak of inflated expectations, the trough of disillusionment, the slope of enlightenment and the plateau of productivity (Fenn & LeHong, 2011). Technologies can be plotted against these phases. The trigger phase documents the steep rise in expectations, with the following phases documenting the peak and inevitable dip as the technology fails to fulfil expectations. The fourth and fifth see a recovery in expectations, but the rise is a gradual one. In practical terms this could be the launch of a new version of the product or a recasting of its purpose. The pace of progression through these phases varies depending on the technology or the product; for technology companies, such a hype cycle can be used to predict the time it will take before the technology will enjoy mainstream adoption.

The lens of 'policy as expectation' emphasises the instrumental or brand-like qualities of a policy idea. Rather than a focus on early adopters, it prompts reflection on the way in which policy-makers are required to 'launch' initiatives as technology companies would launch a gadget or a software update. As illustrated in the previous chapter, one of the common critiques of the Big Society was that it had to be re-launched at least twice. This could be construed as poor policy communication; alternatively, viewed as a technology along a hype cycle, such action is required and, indeed, to be expected.

To summarise, this section has explored three approaches to understanding policy ideas over time, expressed as:

- Policy as activity – measuring fluctuation in frequency
- Policy as diffusion – measuring adoption and realisation
- Policy as expectation – measuring hopes and disillusion

Each approach draws our focus in different directions, to judging policy ideas by counting frequency of activity, or by who has adopted the ideas, or judging expectations in terms of hopes and disillusionment.

Interval frequency is predominant: we know how to count and from this, assumptions are drawn. Measures of frequency of activity offer a convenient and quick means to visualise and get a real-time impression of how a policy idea is faring. But alone they are little more than heuristics. The 'policy as diffusion' model offers insight into who is engaging with policy ideas and when. It also prompts us to find explanations for the role of specific actors, or influencers. It is predominantly agentic, in that it privileges the capacity of actors to shape the outcome of policy ideas. Meanwhile, the 'policy as expectation' model reminds us of the fallibility of policy ideas, that we should be wary of judging success or failure by over inflated expectations and troughs of disillusionment. But at the same time, we need to question the appropriateness of a measure based on the implementation of technologies for application to policy ideas. We need to question the comparability of technologies with policy ideas, since the latter are implemented in predominantly political rather than economic spheres.

Recalling the discussion of empty signifiers in the previous chapter (p. 23), what these models lack is a theory of motivation, a theory of what motivates policy actors to engage with and thereby sustain or curtail the life of policy ideas. The previous chapter argued that they do so through their articulation of demands. This articulation is a form of subscription, and with it comes activity, adoption and expectation. This critique calls for a further model that considers what happens when actors attach diverse demands to existing policy ideas and the equivalences these draw. We require a model that places not just activity, adoption or expectation on the Y axis, but also equivalence.

Policy as equivalence

A fourth approach to tracking policy ideas over time is informed by the work of discourse theorists Laclau and Mouffe (Laclau, 2005; Laclau & Mouffe, 2001). This approach suggests five phases of how a policy idea would develop in terms of the equivalences it draws. The first phase is where ideas are coined and, at their simplest, they are said to be demands. The second phase finds actors articulating other demands, themes, notions and activities as equivalent. The third phase involves a growing chain of precarious equivalences, as more and more is added to what the policy idea 'means'. The resulting forth phase is a hegemonic and almost unquestioned status for the policy idea. The policy idea by now is 'common sense'. The fifth stage is dislocation caused by a range of external factors that make the policy lose its equivalence. These five stages are stylised in Figure 3.4.

A model of 'policy as equivalence' prompts us to question the capacity of policy ideas to accommodate a broad range of demands. It echoes considerations that the appeal of a policy idea can be in its unfinishedness and vagueness: for example, the critique in the previous chapter, that the Big Society was unduly 'meaningless', could be recast as its

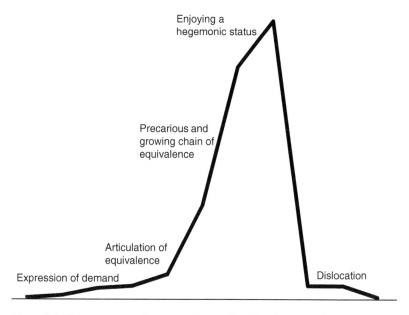

Figure 3.4   Policy as equivalence: tracking policy ideas by equivalence

strength or the source of its appeal. As a policy with a hard identity and yet soft edges, in the case of the Big Society it has been observed that there was a need to maintain room for discretion in order not to appear too paternalistic, which might have led to rejection (Smith, 2010). Not only does the 'policy as equivalence' model capture the container-like character of policy ideas, it is also somewhat attuned to their political nature, their political origins.

What clearly distinguishes the 'policy as equivalence' model for tracing the lifecycle of policy ideas is its offer of a theory of motivation. The conventional assumption is that policy actors will rationally adopt or utilise policy ideas if they see them as furthering their interests (Goldstein & Keohane, 1993). This assumption is perhaps driven by the idea that in policy-making, instrumentalist or opportunistic behaviour is clearly observable; for example a think-tank director who is quick to rebadge their organisation's activities and write an op-ed article soon after the major launch of the policy idea, or the consultant who renames their blog in anticipation of a new policy. However, although such instrumentalist and opportunistic behaviour is widely observable, a theory of motivation purely based on the pursuit of rational interests is insufficient. The alternative theory of motivation, offered by a 'policy as equivalence' model, as to why policy actors coin and foster policy ideas, is explained by a desire for a full and complete identity. The remainder of this section will set out, in theoretical terms, the characteristics and philosophical foundations of this political discourse theory-inspired model, before the final section of the chapter applies the model to the policy idea of Flourishing Neighbourhoods.

The 'policy as equivalence model' argues that policy actors are engaged in a hopeful yet fruitless pursuit of a complete identity. Their goal is to achieve an identity that is unthreatened and fully fledged. Here policy actors are cast as strategic, seeking to hegemonise the terrain they inhabit though hegemonic projects. Policy actors will do this by articulating equivalences and differences and identifying enemies and threats. Identity is based on the recognition of social antagonism, on the identification of an 'other'. However, by basing identity in such a way there will always be the threat and the possibility that their identity could be dislocated. Dislocation is both a traumatic and a productive event. Finally the argument follows that actors are always 'split' in that they cannot, and will not, ever achieve their goal of fullness. This is their failed identity; they have neither complete structural identity nor a complete lack of identity. However, this does not mean that actors do not try to achieve a complete identity or infer that their identity is fully complete. It is the continual attempt to obtain a complete identity that motivates policy actors. As argued previously:

> The idea of closure and fullness still functions as an impossible ideal. Societies are thus organised and centred on the basis of such impossible ideals.
>
> (Howarth & Stavrakakis, 2000, p. 8)

This pursuit of a fully fledged identity results in actors projecting 'completeness' and masking over the gaps. A fully fledged identity entails being certain who the enemy is and therefore interpolating, that is hailing or giving identity to, a certain enemy.

An important logic that is utilised in this process is said to be a logic of fantasy (Howarth et al., 2000). This logic of fantasy helps to symbolise a complete and desirable fullness and certainty, devoid of any threat. However, because there is always a threat, and the wholeness is missing, the logic of fantasy aims to map over this lack through the expression of a fantasmatic logic. Much of this can be found in Lacan's discussion of the difference between reality and the 'Real' (Glynos & Howarth, 2007). In this sense, reality is what agents perceive as the current state of affairs and the Real is what they think it ought to be. Lack is therefore the gap between reality and the Real, or alternatively, the gap between *is* and *ought*. The fantasy logic is about symbolising the lack and alluding to fullness.

In pursuit of their strategic projects, policy actors are engaged in articulating demands, but also in aligning their projects with categories that represent their ideal of a fantasy fullness. It is this role that policy ideas like Flourishing Neighbourhoods or the Big Society play. As policy actors seek to carve out their identities through the expression of political demands, they are attracted to particular policy ideas and are especially drawn to those which represent their ideal of completeness.

To date, the 'policy of equivalence model' based on political discourse theory has been mainly applied to broader political ideas rather than specific policy ideas: it is more likely to be applied to political ideas such as 'democracy', 'green', 'community' or 'race'(Allmendinger, 2005; Lacan, 1982; Stavrakakis, 2012), rather than specific policy ideas, although there are some examples in health and environmental spheres (Howson, 2007; Froud et al., 1998; Griggs & Howarth, 2013).

Political discourse theory-inspired policy work continues to evolve (Budd et al., 2013; Froud et al., 1998; González-Gaudiano, 2005) and increasingly offers a valuable means to understand the role and lifecycle of policy ideas. Scholars are now taking the opportunity to develop what was previously described by Torfing (2005) as a 'young, open, and unfinished research programme ... [where] there is still work to be done' (Carlbom, 2006; Glasze, 2007; Methmann, 2010; Offe, 2009; Torfing, 2005; Wullweber, 2008).

So far, the description of a 'policy as equivalence' model has been without illustration. This final section will now explore the potential of understanding the lifecycle of policy ideas in terms of equivalence and accumulation of meaning, with the example of Birmingham's Flourishing Neighbourhoods.

Lifecycle of Flourishing Neighbourhoods

Flourishing Neighbourhoods is an example of a policy idea observable in public discourse in Birmingham between 2001 and 2004. The analysis presented below draws on documents, agendas, proceedings and newspaper articles, as well as transcribed interviews with policy actors engaged in coining and fostering Flourishing Neighbourhoods. The 'local', delimited nature of this case, both temporally and spatially, is its strength, and offers rare insights into the complete lifecycle of a policy idea.

Tracing the first use of the term Flourishing Neighbourhoods leads us to a group of neighbourhood activists, who had long been arguing that the traditional approach to welfare delivery through a series of organisations and departments was failing their neighbourhood. In seeking a solution they had found a means for a neighbourhood to 'flourish' compared to other areas with similar levels of deprivation. What was evident in their argumentation was that their framing and thinking was explicitly influenced by a range of thinkers and writers who were particularly in vogue at the time in the early 2000s – namely the ideas around communitarianism and social capital (Torfing, 2005).

In many ways the coining of the label for a particular area as a Flourishing Neighbourhoods was relatively inconsequential. But that is the point: policy actors are continually expressing demands that draw on metaphor and analogy and careful use of language. Flourishing Neighbourhoods does this by compounding Flourishing, evoking imagery of organic growth, with Neighbourhood, the preferred label for a locality under the then 'New Labour' government. But careful and creative compounding only goes so far to explain the appeal and emergence of Flourishing Neighbourhoods as a broader policy idea that would become a leitmotiv for policy-making in Birmingham between 2001 and 2004.

It is important to understand the moment at which it was first borrowed by others, beyond the use of neighbourhood activists. In the case of Flourishing Neighbourhoods, it seems the moment of borrowing took place during the preparation for a three day conference in 2001. In designing titles for break-out groups around different policy areas, the conference organisers included a theme for neighbourhood policy that they named: 'Flourishing Neighbourhoods'. On the final day of the conference, known as 'Highbury 3', the organisers designed a newspaper to communicate the various activities. The headline the organisers chose was 'A city of Flourishing Neighbourhoods'. Two forms of translation had taken place: first, the neighbourhood policy discussions were labelled 'Flourishing Neighbourhoods', and second, the classification escalated until Flourishing Neighbourhoods defined the whole conference.

Because borrowing is an act of translation, this means that there is no particular reason why the original demand is considered or maintained. This results in mixed reactions from those making the initial demand. In part it is a story of success, in that their idea for creating better neighbourhoods has caught on, it has been adopted, it has begun to go mainstream. It opens up a range of unforeseen possibilities. But it is also a story of resentment and frustration, in that their demand has been co-opted, corrupted or subverted. Interviewees expressed this in the following ways:

> Flourishing Neighbourhoods is where communities take charge of their own services in their neighbourhood. And that is the ideology...The city council's idea [of Flourishing Neighbourhoods] is no ideology, it is a terminology that says we want to say communities are in control.
>
> (Interview, 2003)

> They [the City Council] stole it [from my friend, he] won't admit it, but he has been pushing it for five years and the City Council have only used it since Highbury 3 [conference in 2001].
>
> (Interview, 2003)

These policy actors in Birmingham were motivated to borrow the term Flourishing Neighbourhoods because of its potential to symbolise their own demands for a city-wide renaissance. In learning why actors were drawn to the idea of adopting Flourishing Neighbourhoods as the main headline for the conference, the organisers recalled a range of reasons:

> Before that evening [of day one of the conference] Flourishing Neighbourhoods was no more prevalent than any other phrase, only that evening did it crystallise...when you have something complex you have to summarise it in some way.
>
> (Interview, 2005)

> We met in the evening and we said the only way we can do this was...to find a slogan which put this together...and Flourishing Neighbourhoods came up...it was clear that the city centre could only survive if the neighbourhoods were flourishing...so it was not only saying the neighbourhoods, it was saying the neighbourhoods *and* the city, as an organic thing, if the neighbourhoods were to be flourishing as well.
>
> (Interview, 2005)

> In choosing the headline I took that phrase because I wanted to have one phrase that made the headline for the newspaper...I think that it had emerged a couple of months before hand... and we picked it up, we thought it would be a possible theme.
>
> (Interview, 2003)

Flourishing Neighbourhoods encapsulated the feelings at the end of day one. Then those involved in the paper production for the Sunday morning took this feeling and made it the headline, the theme for the conference.

(Interview, 2003)

If you could imagine out of a big flipchart comes a discussion sheet...it was a phrase that stuck...I am not sure whose phrase it was, but it was a phrase on the flipchart...that was picked up by media and communications. You can see how these things happen, a team from the City on the Saturday evening brought together all of the notes that had been collected during the day...someone from the media team picked it up and it became an on going notion.

(Interview, 2004)

These quotes offer a rare insight into the birth of a policy idea. So often, the moment of translation remains unknown. In this case, various policy actors offer a broadly consistent account of how Flourishing Neighbourhoods became a headline in the newspaper and the theme that summarised the conference that sought to plan Birmingham's future direction.

Six months after the conference, elite policy actors within the city council labelled their work programme and neighbourhood revitalisation strategy as Flourishing Neighbourhoods. Faced with growing criticism that the ruling administration remained unconcerned about the welfare of their neighbourhoods, it was politically advantageous to underpin their political legacy in urban renaissance by adopting Flourishing Neighbourhoods. With an identity under threat, Flourishing Neighbourhoods symbolised their intent and commitment.

The first public signal of intent came in a newspaper article in late 2001 where the leader of the council expressed how Flourishing Neighbourhoods was his ambition for the city (Dale, 2001, p. 6). Shortly afterwards, there followed a string of comments in the local press about how the consensual message from the conference was about making Birmingham a city of Flourishing Neighbourhoods (Dale, 2001). Between October 2001 and October 2002 it is possible to identify sustained activity that referred consistently to Flourishing Neighbourhoods being part of the city's wider Flourishing Neighbourhood idea, variably expressed, like the Big Society in Chapter 2, as an 'initiative', an 'objective', a 'theme', 'strategy', 'policy' or 'intention' (Lyons, 2001;

Post, 2001). It was formally acknowledged in strategic policy documents such as the Cabinet Statement of 2002 that Flourishing Neighbourhoods was one of three key priorities along with service improvement and devolution. The 'Community Strategy', as the strategic document for the umbrella governance arrangement known as a Local Strategic Partnership, also led with Flourishing Neighbourhoods as part of a vision for Birmingham (BCSP, 2002, p. 5). As a recipient of the then Neighbourhood Renewal Fund, its key strategy document also led with 'Birmingham should become a city recognised for its international competitiveness and celebrated as a city of Flourishing Neighbourhoods' (Partnership, 2002, p. 3).

By 2002 new policies were being legitimised by their connection with Flourishing Neighbourhoods. Examples include the Executive Member for Regeneration proclaiming that the use of Local Finance Improvement Trusts to finance new health facilities 'fits perfectly with the City Council's strategy for creating Flourishing Neighbourhoods' (Hudson, 2002, p. 5).The publicising of a new corporate social responsibility charter for local businesses working with the city was framed as 'a real boost for the City Council's priority to create Flourishing Neighbourhoods' (Connor, 2002, p. 3). When launching the publication of a Crime and Disorder Reduction Strategy, the Deputy Chief Executive was quoted as saying 'we cannot have Flourishing Neighbourhoods unless we can make people feel safer' (Docherty, 2002).

The availability of Flourishing Neighbourhoods offered a clear platform for council actors to articulate new policies, and offered a shorthand for how new entities fit within the existing programme of activity. It helped those communicating the message to make sense and appear consistent to the public reading the stories in their local newspaper. Yet in doing so it also stretched the meaning of Flourishing Neighbourhoods in new directions, into the realms of pragmatic uses alongside Private Finance Initiatives, and well beyond the realms of neighbourhood activism from where it first began. As a policy idea, Flourishing Neighbourhoods had been elevated into the lofty heights of corporate strategy and cross-sectoral engagement.

By 2003, a bewildering range of non-city council policy actors from the social sector, faith groups, charities, businesses and education providers were beginning to brand their activity as Flourishing Neighbourhoods. In workshop discussions and documents Flourishing Neighbourhoods was linked to wider ideas of social capital, well-being and civic pride. It was being linked with terms like generosity, pride, safety and vibrancy. Flourishing Neighbourhoods was being linked

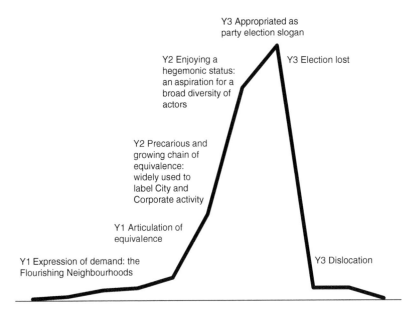

Figure 3.5   Policy as equivalence: example of Flourishing Neighbourhoods
Source: Jeffares 2008.

to everything from library services to racial harmony and cohesive communities.

While on the surface it seemed like a free-for-all in 2003–2004, where anything and everything could be linked to Flourishing Neighbourhoods, there was also a large degree of repetition, with distinct organisations choosing to associate Flourishing Neighbourhoods with community cohesion, or economic prosperity, or investment in suburbs (Figure 3.5).

In the example of Flourishing Neighbourhoods we see two coalitions of actors uniting and attempting to particularise the precarious chain of demands. One coalition was a group that called themselves the 'Flourishing Neighbourhoods Group', a coalition of neighbourhood activists and church leaders who were concerned that demands around morality and humanity were being marginalised in the evolving discussions around Flourishing Neighbourhoods. One member of the group described a seminar where they found the focus of how they wanted to steer the idea of Flourishing Neighbourhoods:

> When the Bishop ... said 'I think Flourishing Neighbourhoods is about generous', you could almost see the light bulbs coming over

people's heads. And the programme was put on one side and people were just discussing 'generous'.

(Interview, 2005)

The group then successfully acquired money from the Single Regeneration Budget and employed a consultant to spend 18 months researching and preparing a report that would set out a manifesto for Flourishing Neighbourhoods in line with their view.

During the same period another set of actors – the Labour group – at that point in control of the city council, were increasingly losing ground in the polls; the Labour Government were threatening to invade Iraq, Birmingham had failed to transfer its social housing to the social sector, and the city was rated 'Weak' by the Audit Commission's Corporate Performance Assessment. There was a risk that Labour would lose control of the city at the next election, a city it had held for two decades. With such a loss went the legacy of renaissance that politicians and their closest officials had cultivated, Birmingham's new-found international reputation and a renaissance of the city centre that pointed back to memories of the 'best governed city in the world'. Flourishing Neighbourhoods offered an opportunity, and became an aspiration of the Labour group. Flourishing Neighbourhoods became the main slogan of the Labour group's 2004 election campaign.

Although Labour retained the most seats at the local election, they lost control to a Conservative-Liberal Democrat coalition. But crucially for the fate of Flourishing Neighbourhoods, its new-found particularity and association with Labour meant that anything branded Flourishing Neighbourhoods was abolished by the new coalition. All city council-related activity and documents carrying Flourishing Neighbourhoods were rebranded as Vibrant Villages.

It may seem from the case of Flourishing Neighbourhoods that certain policy actors have agency or a capacity to control policy ideas. While it is the case that, once in train, certain policy actors can help promote policy ideas through the strategic application of resources, the subsequent failure of Vibrant Villages to be widely adopted reminds us that they cannot simply be coined and disseminated overnight.

This case study of Flourishing Neighbourhoods demonstrates how policy actors do often have the capacity, compared to less powerful coalitions, to particularise precarious chains. The temptation to do so clearly can be overwhelming. But as the Labour group found after they adopted Flourishing Neighbourhoods as an election slogan, to do so can be to kill the golden goose.

Conclusion

This chapter provocatively began on a somewhat morbid note with a focus on death. So often the question levelled at policy ideas is – why does an idea 'catch on'? Kingdon, for example captures this nicely:

> Gradually, the idea catches on. People in and around government speak of a 'growing realisation', 'an increased feeling', a 'lot of talk in the air', and 'coming to conclusion'. After some degree of diffusion, there seems to be a take-off point: many people are discussing the proposal or idea. At that point, knowledgeable people refer to a 'widespread feeling,' ... by now it is orthodox thinking.
>
> (Kingdon, 1995, p. 140)

The appeal of Kingdon's argument is that we seldom question policy ideas once they are taken for granted. This chapter, by starting instead with a focus on death, revealed the difficulty of certifying the death of policy and therefore the challenge of understanding lifecycles. It is a curious state of affairs that these inventions of policy actors command so much attention and resources and yet there is relatively little understanding of how, why and when policy actors move from one policy idea to the next.

The challenge of understanding the lifecycle of policy ideas led to exploration of four possible models of tracking policy over time. The first, a focus on activity, is perhaps the most recognisable from policy textbooks. It appeals to an intuition to judge the health of a policy idea in terms of fluctuating activity. Technology provides exciting opportunities to visualise activity in the same vein as suggested by Downs or Parsons. Models of policy as diffusion and as expectation were also highlighted, but offer limited insight mainly because policy ideas, as political entities, are so much more than technological products.

The chapter then outlined and illustrated a fourth and alternative approach, measuring 'policy as equivalence', offering with it a theory of motivation of policy actors, and sketched how prominent policy ideas can be stable, popular and taken for granted one day and then dislocated and redundant the next. This reminds us that launching and promoting a policy idea makes it vulnerable.

The policy as equivalence model was illustrated through the case of Flourishing Neighbourhoods, demonstrating how in less than 1,000 days a policy idea can dominate the political landscape of a large British city and fade to obscurity. While not every idea follows such a path, it offers us a starting point for further enquiry in later chapters of this book.

Both Flourishing Neighbourhoods and the Big Society, discussed in Chapter 2, are policy ideas with identifiable sponsors, and their 'launch' can be pin-pointed to a particular date. Both enjoyed considerable attention for several months, before being acknowledged as 'dead' in media discussion. (for a comparison of the two policy ideas, see Table 9.1 in the Appendix). The gap between the formal launch and the death notice in each case was a notably comparable 30 months, although at the time of writing the Big Society continues to be an official policy of the Coalition Government. It would be tempting, but overly simplistic, to argue that policy ideas tend to live for 1,000 days.

However, what separates Flourishing Neighbourhoods, coined in 2001, and the Big Society, coined in 2009, as policy ideas, aside from scale and scope, is eight years. The eight years that separate these policy ideas was a time of rapid technological advancement. It was a period that some acknowledge as a transition from web1.0 to web2.0, in terms of access and use of the internet, and the arrival of social media platforms such as Twitter, Facebook, YouTube and mobile computing on smart phones and tablets.

This leads us to new questions about how policy ideas live in this 'new' environment (Docherty, 2002). The temptation is to say that the arrival of new social media platforms, which give citizens, voters and a plethora of policy actors a new-found capacity to comment and publish, introduces a new kind of environment for policy ideas. To understand how policy ideas fare in a web2.0 context requires further study and methodological innovation. Later chapters in this book will seek to respond to these challenges; first, however, it is important to explore the best means of understanding how viewpoints come to emerge around policy ideas, and how best to capture this process.

4
Identifying Policy Viewpoints

With definitions of policy ideas and their lifecycles now in place, this chapter explores how to map the viewpoints surrounding policy ideas by considering the example of Total Place (Grint & Holt, 2011; H. M. Treasury, 2010). The chapter explores the importance of capturing early conversations surrounding a policy idea, and discusses the implications for later stages of its lifecycle. Capturing and mapping this subjectivity requires a sensitive and systematic method. The method applied in this chapter is called Q methodology, a long-established technique in psychology and behavioural science which is of growing interest to public policy research.

The chapter is structured in three sections. The first briefly introduces the policy idea of Total Place and gives an overview of the research principles of Q methodology, and then sets out a Q methodology research design for capturing and mapping the shared viewpoints surrounding Total Place. The second section reports the results of a study that revealed four shared viewpoints about Total Place. The analysis reports the character of these viewpoints and what distinguishes them. It explores which policy actors informed these viewpoints and their justifications for their views. The credibility of a Q methodology research design rests on the ability of researchers to sample the diversity of subjectivity surrounding a topic, requiring exposure to its total communicability, that is the total volume of debate surrounding an issue. In Q methodology this total volume of debate is known as the 'concourse' (Stephenson, 1978).

The third section of the chapter critically reflects on the growth of Q methodology in public policy research and its capacity to credibly capture the concourse of debate surrounding policy topics. It concludes by arguing that, although current approaches used in Q policy studies are by and large comprehensive, they are resource intensive, and there are questions around the suitability of techniques like Q methodology in an era of social media where discussion of policy is increasingly high volume and high velocity.

Designing viewpoint research

Total Place was announced in April 2009, the final year of Brown's Labour administration. Building on previous studies in three English counties – Cumbria, Norfolk and Suffolk (Local Leadership Centre, 2009), Total Place was a policy idea adopted and fostered by Lord Bichard as part of his contribution to the Treasury's Operational Efficiency Programme. Total Place was about 'mapping total public spend in a local area and identifying efficiencies through local public sector collaboration' (H. M. Treasury, 2009, p. 12). In 2009 the government sponsored pilot projects in 13 localities; these Total Place pilots were established with the aim of exploring means of substantially improving public policy outcomes at a local level and at lower cost to the public purse. The pilot projects were encouraged to foster local innovation and collaboration. Members of each of the pilots met for the first time in August 2009. A timeline for Total Place can be summarised as follows:

- April 2009: Policy announced in the Budget (H. M. Treasury, 2009)
- August 2009: 13 Pilots meet
- September 2009: Pilots contribute analysis of 'Total Public Spend' for pre-budget statement
- February 2010: Pilots deliver reports to Treasury
- March 2010: Treasury publishes final report (H. M. Treasury, 2010)
- May 2010: General election, Labour loses power
- June 2010: Policy actors responsible for Total Place publically acknowledge that the policy idea has been terminated
- November 2010: Total Place website closes down, with comment that 'learning' from Total Place will inform a policy of Community Budgets.

By May 2010, the future of Total Place was in question. This was despite the fact that seven months earlier, when 13 pilots were up and running, Lord Bichard was confident enough to state that 'Total Place is not just another Whitehall initiative' (Local Leadership Centre, 2009). This was also despite the fact that in March, the Treasury and Department for Communities and Local Government had jointly published their final report (H. M. Treasury, 2010) documenting the activities of the pilot projects. Yet, following the creation of a new Conservative–Liberal Democrat coalition government, it was left to Bichard to concede that he did not think the Total Place 'brand will survive' (Public Property, 2010). Instead, he suggested that the Total Place emphasis might remain in some other form under a Conservative–Liberal Democrat coalition government. The new local government minister expressed his unremitting sympathy and support for Total Place, and hinted of a change in brand and focus: 'Whatever we call the next generation of Total Place, it has to be about outcomes' (Bob Neill, quoted in LocalGov, 2010). During 2010 the government set out plans for a pilot programme called 'Community Budgets'.

To recall from the previous chapter's discussion of Flourishing Neighbourhoods and the Big Society, certifying the death of a policy idea is a difficult task. Many of the actors involved in Total Place subsequently became involved in the successive policy idea of Community Budgets. For some involved, Total Place was by no means viewed as new or original, recalling as it did various previous policy ideas for local government: Single Regeneration Budget; City Challenge; New Deal for Communities; Neighbourhood Renewal Fund; Best Value; or Local Area Agreements. It is not about mourning the loss of a brand name. Not everybody will share this view. There were others working within the Total Place pilot projects that viewed Total Place as a unique and distinctive policy idea. The associations and meaning attached to a policy idea are a matter of inter-subjective viewpoint.

A systematic method for understanding the nuanced inter-subjective viewpoints surrounding a policy idea is Q methodology. Q methodology (from here on 'Q') was first developed by British-born psychologist William Stephenson in the 1930s, and elaborated in his book *The Study of Behavior* (1953). For public policy research the contribution of Q for understanding political subjectivity was consolidated in the book *Political Subjectivity* (1980), by one of Stephenson's graduate students Steven Brown, who had introduced Q to policy research in earlier work (Coke & Brown, 1976). Over the last three decades Q has been increasingly applied to a wide range of topics by researchers across the social and human sciences, being particularly strong in health and education research and in work on environmental science and health economics (Baker et al., 2006).

It is becoming increasingly clear that public policy research has also discovered the contribution of Q methodology (Brown et al., 2008; Day, 2008). Policy researchers are drawn to Q for its ability to map subjectivity surrounding a policy problem or proposed solution. They find that Q helps to reveal the topology of shared viewpoints, their character, distinctiveness and inter-relationships.

Durning (1999) suggests five areas of public policy research where Q can, and has, played a role including: identifying policy preferences, understanding stakeholder interests, defining policy problems, informing policy evaluation and capturing multiple moral judgements.

Q helps identify the preferences of different groups and their perspectives on policy proposals. Published examples include exploration around discourses of support and objection to wind farms (Ellis et al., 2007), aircraft noise (Kroesen & Bröer, 2009), to the planning of nuclear power facilities (Venables et al., 2009), or waste infrastructure (Wolsink, 2004). Q is also used to understand 'stakeholder interests', with examples attempting to reveal the 'democratic software' of those working in or designing hybrid governance arrangements (Mathur & Skelcher, 2007; Skelcher et al., 2013); or to explore the motivations behind travel choices (van Exel et al., 2011), bear conservation (Rutherford et al., 2009), civil aviation (Van Eeten, 2001) or forest management (Steelman & Maguire, 1999).

Q is used to explore the multiple definitions of emerging policy problems, and previous work has focused on everything from 'war on terror' to HIV, from pandemic influenza to climate change (Callahan et al., 2006; Hoppe, 2009; Niemeyer et al., 2005; Prasad, 2001; Prateepko & Chongsuvivatwong, 2009).

Q has also been applied to policy evaluation, to help understand the value or efficiency of policies (Dickinson et al., 2013), and helped inform work requiring moral judgement, where there are multiple meanings of 'fair' in terms of judging policy alternatives (de Graaf & van Exel, 2008): for example, it has been used to explore end-of-life care (Wong et al., 2004), and how best to allocate scarce health budgets (Baker, 2006).

To summarise, Q research seeks to capture the diversity of communication surrounding a topic to identify the presence of shared viewpoints; it is the scientific study of inter-subjectivity. Stephenson described the diversity of debate, or total communicability surrounding a topic, as the 'concourse' of debate (Stephenson, 1978). By asking respondents engaged with a topic to perform a Q sort, that is, a standardised and modified ranking procedure, based on a sample of items portraying this concourse, the Q sorts of these respondents can be correlated, factorised and underlying viewpoints revealed. The viewpoints are then interpreted for their character and distinctiveness and illustrated with insights from those respondents who inform and exemplify each viewpoint. This section will now illustrate these procedures further by applying Q to reveal viewpoints surrounding the policy idea of Total Place.

The first task in the application of Q to this matter is to capture the concourse of debate emanating from those working amidst the Total Place policy idea. Some of this can be found in reports and newspaper articles, but may also be drawn from the interaction between actors at meetings, workshops and in email exchanges. The aim of assessing this concourse is to capture expressions of opinion about the policy, in terms of working definitions, evaluations, hopes and prescriptions. The aim of the first phase of this process is to capture these expressions in the form of a set of short statements known as Q statements.

To capture the concourse of debate, my collaborator Martin Willis and I attended meetings and workshops of one of the 13 Total Place pilot projects, and also collected working papers, reports and newspaper articles (further details of this process can be found in the Appendix and in Willis & Jeffares, 2012). Some of the richest sources of Q statements included emails, press releases, workshop debates, consultation events, presentation slides and flip chart notes. We conducted interviews with policy actors leading projects that included representatives from local public agencies, external consultants and members of the social sector. Over a two month collection phase (November–December 2009) the aim was to collect the broadest possible selection of material for sampling into a smaller set that could be administered to research participants as a Q sort. We collected a total of 221 potential Q statements.

Because of the limitations of how many statements a respondent is able to rank order, Q methodologists are required to devise a system for producing a 'manageable' Q set of around 35 to 50 statements, while trying as best as possible to retain the diversity of debate. Not everything needs to be retained: as Watts and Stenner put it, the task is something akin to carpeting a room with carpet tiles. Tiles should be retained at the edge of the debate as well as at the centre, but on no account should you attempt to cover every inch of the floor (Watts & Stenner, 2012, p. 61). Unless the topic area is already highly structured by a particular theoretical model, Q researchers sample statements by using a balanced block sampling frame (Fisher, 1971) whereby potential statements are placed into a grid to ensure a balance in the statements. The process of sampling is designed to reveal and strip out any duplicates and ensure there is something for everyone in the final set.

In sampling statements, the aim is not to ensure that every statement is meaningful to everybody taking part, but rather to ensure that each statement is at least meaningful to somebody. At this stage it is permissible to merge and combine statements provided the natural language is retained. Some statements will be short – just four or five words – while others could be longer strings, or one or two sentences. Some Q methodologists try to keep the statements short and simple in the hope of controlling for meaning, but as this is an interpretive process whereby the object of the study is to understand how the same thing can mean different things to different people, then such attempts are ill-founded. Q methodology is particularly attuned to how a statement can mean different things to the same person under different conditions. A person can cycle home shouting at car drivers and then get into their car and proceed to shout at the cyclists. Subjectivity is operant, dependent on context.

To sample our 221 potential statements for the Total Place study, we adapted a framework advocated by Janet Newman in her study of governance (Newman, 2001). Newman describes how her framework, for in her case, mapping government modernisation, built on the work of Quinn (1991), who 'developed a framework for mapping the contradictions in organisation life, identifying four different models or approaches: the rational goal approach, the developmental or open systems approach, the consensual or team approach, and the hierarchical or internal process approach' (Newman, 2001, p. 33). Newman mapped these approaches on two axes, with the vertical axis representing decentralised to centralised, and the horizontal axis representing a continuum from continuity to change. Plotted on a matrix, Newman shows how this offers four positions, or as she develops the approach, four 'tensions': 'self-governance', 'open systems', 'hierarchy' and 'rational goal'. We found these four labels a useful starting point to distinguish our Total Place statements.

1. Self-governance – Citizen empowerment
2. Open systems – Partnership
3. Hierarchy – Authority
4. Rational goal – Economic rational

We reviewed our set of potential statements one by one using our sampling framework. Statements that were placed in cell 1, 'self-governance', reflected sentiments of how Total Place presented opportunities for bottom-up, citizen-focused governance. Statements in cell 2, 'open systems' represented the potential of Total Place for partnership working and network governance. Statements in cell 3, 'hierarchy', discussed the potential for Total Place to reassert bureaucracy, leadership and authority. Statements in cell 4, 'rational goal', tended to emphasise ideas of realising cost savings, efficiencies and performance management. We also found statements that anticipated the possible outcomes of Total Place. Rather than sort these into the four Newman–Quinn inspired cells, we added two additional outcome cells.

5. Outcome for cultural change
6. Outcome for consumer citizen

In cell 5, we included outcome statements around ideas of cultural change. In cell 6, we placed statements discussing the potential beneficial outcomes for consumers and citizens. These two outcome cells reflected a common concern of Total Place policy actors they couched in terms of three C's: 'customer', 'cost' and 'culture' (Brindle, 2009).

The 221 potential Q statements were sorted into the six cells of the sampling framework. During sampling, duplicates and ambiguous statements were discarded. The aim was to have a balanced block of seven statements in each cell to produce a final Q set of 42 statements. (A full list of this final Q set can be found in the Appendix p. 149, Table 9.2). We piloted the statements with five colleagues to clarify and refine the language. Although we attempted to develop a representative set of statements, ultimately we agree with Brown, that whatever we as investigators consider a balanced set, it is ultimately the respondent that bestows meaning to the statements through the process of sorting (Brown, 1993). Q is more than just 'getting out what you put in'. It is not about deductively testing to see if the sampling themes are reflected in the results; instead the sampling framework should be understood as nothing more than a disposable heuristic. As an heuristic, the sampling framework is used to help ensure the diversity of the debate is represented in the Q set. Post-sort, the heuristic is ultimately redundant, in that it is superseded by the sorting preferences of the respondents.

Once Q methodologists have finalised their Q set they then set about administering Q sorts to a set of respondents. The saturation point of most Q studies is closer to 50 than it is to 100. Q studies require only enough respondents to reveal the limit of shared viewpoints. While the almost infinite combination of rankings will mean everybody would express a unique sort, the interest in Q is revealing where shared viewpoints have emerged, that is, where Q sorts are correlated. Therefore, many successful Q studies employ between 45 and 70 respondents.

As Brown puts it, 'In such a study, one quickly reaches the point where the testimony of great numbers of additional informants provides no further validation. Who bows to whom and when, for instance, needs no statistical study of all Japan' (Brown, 1980, p. 194).

The established means of administering a Q sort is in a face-to-face interview, although there are alternative means. There is no denying that a one-on-one Q sort interview is the most revealing means to collect Q sorts. It ensures that the participant is supported through the process, minimising erroneous sorting, and the researcher is able to watch the process and engage in a post-sort conversation. The empathy achieved during a Q sort interview needs, however, to be balanced with the time and resources it takes to recruit, set up and conduct interviews. The alternative for many years has either been to post out packs of cards and instructions, to conduct Q sorts over the telephone or administer Q sorts en masse in locations such as classrooms or conference halls.

For the last 20 years several attempts have been made to exploit the opportunity for online Q sorts. The challenge has always been how to replicate the sorting experience of a Q sort interview remotely on a screen. Pioneers were Web-Q and Q Sorter (Q Method, 2013), followed by Solitaire Q, FlashQ and Q-Assessor. Byung Lee's Solitaire Q was ground-breaking in that it introduced a drag and drop interface, and Brehler and Hackert followed soon after in 2007 with FlashQ (Hackert & Braehler, 2007) a freeware tool that researchers could host on their own Linux server.

The Total Place study used FlashQ (Hackert & Braehler, 2007). Potential respondents are sent an email with a web link. The link was circulated by the Total Place partnership organisations and 40 responses were collected online. A further 24 were collected using FlashQ on laptops setup in the foyer of a Total Place conference, giving a total of 64. The 64 respondents spent an average of 24 minutes completing the online Q sort, including writing a short passage about the reason for choosing their two most and two least agreeable statements. No identifying information was collected, although we did ask respondents about their organisational affiliation and job status (see p. 151).

Although self-selecting, Table 9.3 shows respondents were suitably diverse for a Q study (where issues of representation fall on the Q set rather than the person sample), with just over half working for the local authority and a good spread of frontline, middle manager and senior professionals.

Respondents were given one condition of instruction: 'to what extent do you find the following descriptions of Total Place agree with your

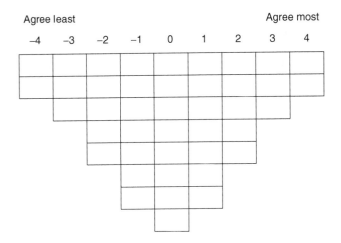

Figure 4.1   Total Place Q sorting grid

point of view?' After clicking the invitation link, participants were shown the 42 statements in a random order and were instructed to place them either on an 'Agree' pile, a 'Disagree' pile, or if not sure or indifferent, they placed the statement on a third 'Neutral pile'. After sorting all 42 statements, they were then presented with a sorting grid that ran from agree most to agree least. The highest degree of agreement was +4 and the lowest −4. To populate the grid, participants were then asked to sort through the agree pile and choose the two statements they agreed with the most, allocate them under the +4 column and then continue until the grid was complete (see Figure 4.1).

Four viewpoints of Total Place

Using PQMethod, the analysis of the Total Place Q sorts revealed a four-factor solution (see Appendix, Table 9.2).

Within this solution, three statements were judged consensus statements, in that they did not significantly distinguish between any pairs of factors. These consensus statements included those that saw Total Place as a way of making upstream investment to save downstream costs (statement 21), and the idea of creating dialogue between, and using the skills of, different sectors (statements 26, 40). These consensus statements were placed indifferently by all four factors.

In the process of interpretation, we began to compare four aspects. First, we focused on clues to how the viewpoint imagined or experienced the current governance environment. Second, we focused on how Total Place was portrayed within this imagined governance environment. Third, we noted outcome aspirations for the Total Place activity. Fourth, we identified discussion of levers and barriers enabling or impeding this aspiration for Total Place. To identify images, hopes, levers and barriers we focused on how statements were prioritised within each factor array (see Appendix, Table 9.2) and additional written text offered by respondents whose sorts closely resembled or exemplified the shared viewpoint – these respondents are known as 'exemplars'.

The four viewpoints were labelled People-Centred, Knowledge Leadership, Total Place Vision and Strategic Direction. Below, we report the characteristics of our four viewpoints, including quotes from viewpoint exemplars.

Viewpoint 1: Total Place 'People-Centred'

> People at the grassroots level and on the frontline are the people with the knowledge… We have spent too much time developing services that we think communities need, and not enough time ensuring that the services that are available are relevant to the people who need support.
>
> (Respondent 41)

Image of governance

This 'people-centred' viewpoint argues that successful governance is that which prioritises local people in the design and development of services (statement 38) and gives people what they need, in the way they want it (31). There is a strong emphasis on localism with 'local agendas' being developed for 'local neighbourhoods' with staff from 'local agencies' working together, managed by empowered 'local managers who control resources locally'. It expresses doubts around the leadership potential of politicians (6) and worries about top down control (2).

Image of Total Place

From this starting perspective, Total Place is viewed as a new and distinct idea (14) which requires organisational culture change (10). It does not see financial analysis as being the most critical dimension (17).

Hopes and aspirations

Total Place is viewed as having the potential to deliver a different kind of people-centred public service, which addresses the whole person and gives people what they need, in the way they want it (31, 32) and all within a changed organisational culture (10).

Levers/barriers

For Total Place to work well, this grouping suggests that actors in the process require an inquisitive understanding of customers (33), focusing on the whole person rather than the presenting problem (32). Potentially disruptive forces would pertain if Total Place was viewed as social engineering (39) or if it was allowed to be driven by politicians rather than local officials (6).

Viewpoint 2: Total Place through Knowledge Leadership

> We know, or at least ought to know what services we provide . . . We have this information. It may be here there and everywhere at the moment but we have it, and from this we can highlight gaps and duplication.
>
> (Respondent 60)

Image of governance

This *knowledge leadership* viewpoint emphasises leadership for whole systems change (8), organisational culture change (10) and achieving more for less (20) through using existing joint intelligence and shared analysis (5). As one exemplar argued: 'Total Place is about a cross-sector collaboration to understand and meet the needs of local people and agree and share priorities for using resources to improve lives in the future'. Conversely, this grouping does not see Total Place as leading to more central control (2) or, for that matter, as an opportunity for grass roots action (13).

Image of Total Place

Total Place is viewed as 'ensuring joined up, integrated services across statutory, public and voluntary sectors delivering services tailored to residents' needs'. It is about local authorities and other public services 'getting their own houses in order', by eliminating duplication and providing a more efficient, and ultimately more beneficial, public service.

Hopes and aspirations

Success for Total Place would be found in 'whole systems change' (8), and new organisational cultures (10) using existing knowledge and moving towards a single performance framework for local government, health and police.

Levers/barriers

Total Place will be delivered as a result of effective leadership (8) and shared intelligence (5) and would be undermined if it did not draw on existing knowledge and understanding (12). Progress towards realising Total Place could also be disrupted by agencies devolving too much to the frontline (13) or giving citizens the power to decide how money is spent (36).

Viewpoint 3: Total Place Vision

> 80% of budgets are spent on 20% of users – and there may be duplication and hence waste where many agencies are involved. A more joined up holistic approach would address this.
>
> (Respondent 52)

Image of governance

This viewpoint reflects an optimistic belief that Total Place is a unique approach that can make a real difference. It argues that governance will require a new statutory responsibility for agencies to work together (23), and jointly analysing intelligence (5). They do not support central control because, as one respondent stated, 'it has been demonstrated to fail and will not lead to the innovation needed'.

Image of Total Place

Here Total Place begins with a strong focus on high-cost users (27) with an understanding that 'reducing high costs can bring quick wins which will generate commitment to taking things further'. There is a firm emphasis on working together in that it 'needs everyone to have joint responsibility...unless a single pot [is] dedicated to the whole, it will not work'.

Hopes and aspirations

Therefore, Total Place requires leadership which delivers whole systems change (8). It will dramatically reduce overall expenditure through focusing on high-cost users and breaking recurring patterns (27) thereby preventing future problems (25).

Levers/barriers

Paradoxically this group emphasises statutory collaboration (23) and joint intelligence (5) but rejects more central control (2). In relation to finances, Total Place is about achieving more for less with reduced expenditure on high-cost users, but it disagrees with realising cashable efficiencies by decommissioning services (19) or the idea that Total Place is about one public service budget being spent by another public service (28).

Viewpoint 4: Total Place as Strategic Direction

Image of governance

Like Viewpoint 2, this *strategic direction* view does not believe that giving power to citizens (36) or frontline staff (13) is the best way forward. However, it differs in terms of regarding current knowledge as insufficient, both in terms of 'the needs and expectations of people' and 'what works for the people of the area and why' (9). They are the only group to consider Total Place as being about central control, and stress the importance of leadership, cultural change and statutory collaboration.

Image of Total Place

This image of Total Place is a policy idea promoting leadership for whole systems change (8) and a statutory responsibility to tackle issues together (23). It believes this will enable a focus on high-cost users (27) and the achievement of 'more for less' (20).

Hopes and aspirations

This group do not see Total Place as primarily concerned with community/citizen outcomes or empowerment. Indeed, it is the only group to explicitly reject the notion that Total Place is an opportunity to promote diversity and a multicultural society (29). The priority for this group is 'about delivering good public services' based on 'high level, strategic service redesign'.

Levers and barriers

The key levers here are seen as leadership (8) and statutory collaboration (23) whilst the potential barriers are bottom-up forces of citizen power (36) and giving too much autonomy to the frontline (13).

Comparison of the viewpoints

Across the four viewpoints, the image of existing governance arrangements suggests some areas of consensus. For instance, three of the
viewpoints prioritise joined up working. However, these vary both
in the strength and the locus of collaboration. Thus whilst Viewpoints 2 and 3 emphasise joint intelligence (5), Viewpoints 3 and 4
both go further in suggesting the need for legislation to encourage
effective joint working (23). In contrast, Viewpoint 1 stresses a focus
on customers' needs (31, 32, 33, 38) with little regard for partnership
statements.

In terms of images of Total Place in itself, views range from Viewpoint 4, where Total Place is seen as a strategic initiative, to the optimism
demonstrated in Viewpoint 1's view that Total Place opens up opportunities for bottom-up, co-production (38). This contrasts with the view
of Viewpoints 2 and 4, where they disagree with the notion of citizens
being given the power to decide how money is spent (36). Viewpoints 3
and 4 share a focus on high-cost users (27) with Viewpoint 3's vision
presaging a preventative agenda (25).

Compared with what are divergent images of Total Place, the outcome aspirations are more consensual across the four viewpoints. All
four viewpoints associate Total Place with changing organisational culture (10), leadership for whole systems change (8) and achieving 'more
for less' with the public purse (20). However, differences emerge in relation to the emphasis on outcomes for individuals and communities,
which are important for Viewpoint 1 but notably less so for the other
three viewpoints.

There is broad agreement across the four viewpoints as to what would
enable, or indeed prevent, Total Place from succeeding. For example,
all four viewpoints share a belief, albeit with varying strength, in the
importance of an inquisitive understanding of what makes customers
tick (33). And again, all groups do not support the view of one service
being able to spend the budget allocated to another service.

But overall, there remain many differences. Contrast for example
Viewpoint 1's priority for customer choice and control (31), with
Viewpoint 2's confidence in existing knowledge, and Viewpoint 3's ide-
alistic belief in prevention. Conversely, Viewpoint 4 is characterised
by its emphasis on strategic leadership and the potentially negative
consequences of empowering citizens or frontline staff.

So far this chapter has applied Q methodology to the policy idea of
Total Place by capturing policy actor discussion of policy actors involved

in the policy idea. The views expressed around the policy were sampled and shared with the policy actors using an online 'Q sort' where they were asked to rank the statements in order of agreement with their current view of the Total Place policy idea.

The example shows how four distinct viewpoints were emerging, with Viewpoint 3 perhaps most closely resembling the intention of the policy idea's original sponsor. But the question becomes how, over time, this viewpoint accommodates the other three distinct viewpoints. Viewpoint 4, for example, is focused on strategic direction and has little regard for the contribution from frontline or community groups or voluntary organisations. In contrast Viewpoint 1 identifies the role of communities and people to help to deliver and co-produce solutions.

This example has illustrated how policy actors not only invest considerable resources in coining and fostering policy ideas; they are also engaged in nuanced games of meaning. It has shown that as the idea diffuses beyond its original sponsors, so the concourse surrounding the policy idea grows. The flurry of activity during this period of emergence obscures the parallel emergence of tacit, or at least variably acknowledged, divergent viewpoints.

At this point in the process, these differences remain implicit. The policy actors engaging in the workshops, conferences and the authorship of op-ed articles and blogs are far from antagonistic. At this point in the process, Total Place has the capacity to accommodate everybody. But there are weak points, where differences will emerge.

This chapter takes us beyond asking whether or not an idea is genuinely new or any sense that such ideas are too 'nebulous' to be subjected to rigorous analysis. But there are limitations. The strength of using Q methodology to interpret implicit and sometimes tacit intersubjectivity in the formative stages of policy ideas depends on the ability of researchers using Q methodology to credibly capture the diversity of debate across a range of places and platforms. To do so is resource intensive. The example here of Total Place required special permission to grant access to meetings and conferences in order to capture the 'on stage' discussion of the policy idea. It is not so simple to capture the 'off stage' discussion that takes place in lunch queues, drinks after work and email exchange. There are also questions of whether such an approach is sufficient to capture the temporal diversity of concourse (Wolf, 2004). With these possibilities and limitations in mind, the third and final section of this chapter turns to focus on how public policy research can best incorporate Q methodology into its work.

Assessing policy concourse

Public policy researchers go to considerable lengths to evaluate the concourse, that is the volume or breadth of debate surrounding the topic in question and to develop a set of statements for Q sorting that is representative of the character and diversity of such a debate. To illustrate the range of current approaches, Table 4.1 highlights some recently published policy oriented Q studies. The following section considers these five in terms of their research design, how they capture the diversity of discussion and sample from this concourse.

In the first example, Steelman and Maguire (1999) report two distinct accounts of using Q to understand stakeholder priorities. Their study seeks to understand residents' priorities for ecosystem management by drawing on beliefs and values. The Q study is described as an extension of a large qualitative project drawing on 143 resident interviews and additional written responses. This archive forms the source of statements. Although the authors label their approach to sampling as 'unstructured', they report using five category 'issue areas' (forests, wildlife, roads, water, recreation) based on common topics raised in the original interviews. Rather than overt attempts to balance equal numbers of statements across each category, the authors allow the balance to reflect priorities of the residents, where possible balancing to ensure neither pro nor con viewpoints are overrepresented. A total of 55 statements formed the final Q set.

In a second example, David Ockwell (Ockwell, 2008) explores stakeholder perspectives of fire in the Cape York area of Australia. Ockwell cites Brown's notion of concourse as the volume of discussion or population of viewpoints (Brown, 1986). Ockwell derives his understanding of the concourse from a mixture of literature and face-to-face consultation with people that have a stake, or an interest, in fire in Cape York over a four year period. He acknowledges that this approach neglects exposure to indigenous community accounts and supplements this by using proceedings of two conferences, two seminars and eight published works spanning 1975–2000. He reports that 304 statements were collected and narrowed to 36 using a 16 cell sampling matrix developed by Dryzek and Berejikian in their study of democratic discourses in the USA (Dryzek & Berejikian, 1993). The matrix includes four types of claim (based on Toulmin, 1958): definitive, designative, evaluative and advocative, and four 'discourse elements': ontology, agency, motivations and relationships.

Table 4.1 Examples of concourse development in policy research

Study	Source	Sampling	Result
Steelman and Maguire Resident priorities for ecosystem management	Earlier research project – 143 interviews plus	Unstructured, thematic, (5 inductive themes)	68 Q sorts, administered by mail
Steelman and Maguire to explore five aspects of current plan – most useful aspects, what works, public perception, purpose involvement, who to involve	Focus group with 15 employees	Opportunistic	15 Q sorts, five separate sorts of Q sets ranging from 11 to 26 items
Ockwell – exploring stakeholder perceptions of fire in Cape York Australia	Earlier/parallel research project, 'face to face consultation', transcripts and proceedings of 2 seminars/2 conferences, 8 published works of indigenous community perspectives	Structured, 4 × 4 discourse/claim structure, allowing 304 statements to be reduced to 36.	32 Q sorts, administered through email

Table 4.1 (Continued)

Study	Source	Sampling	Result
De Graaf 2011 – exploring public administrator loyalties	Academic and popular literature	Thematic (7 themes) based on existing models, allowing 600 quotes to be reduced to 42	
Cuppen – values and beliefs surrounding biomass	Stakeholder dialogue transcripts (previous study), reports and newspaper articles	Iterative categories of three researchers, to identify agreed categories and unique statements, piloting for coherence and omissions with 5 people allowed 200 potential statements to be reduced to 62.	75 sorts, administered via interview
Jeffares and Skelcher – democratic subjectivities of public administrators working in governance networks	Published books and articles, interview transcripts from earlier projects	3×3 grid based on the 4×4 used by Ockwell and devised by Dryzek (definitions, opinions, prescriptions) and (relationships, agency and motivation) and balanced across a published typology (Klijn and Skelcher, 2007). 300 potential statements reduced to Q set of 36.	49 sorts administered online using FlashQ

In a third example, a study by de Graaf concerns the loyalties of public administrators (de Graaf, 2010). His conception of concourse draws on Brown (1980).

> It is best to use a structure for selection of a representative miniature of such a list. Whatever structure is used it forces the investigator to select statements widely different from one another in order to make the Q-set broadly representative.
>
> (de Graaf, 2010, p. 8, citing Brown, 1980, p. 8)

De Graaf reports collecting 600 quotes describing loyalties, responsibilities and role connections from academic and popular literature. To sample statements, the researcher devised a sampling matrix of seven categories based on the frameworks of leading scholars in this field (Bovens, 1998; Petter, 2005), the categories being – hierarchical, personal, social, professional, societal, legal and customer loyalty. The sampling ensured a balance between 'thick and thin' examples of loyalty, although this is only partially defined as the object and the background of each type of loyalty.

In describing his sampling strategy, de Graaf is at pains to point out that a different set of statements drawn from the sample would most likely converge on the same conclusion (citing Thomas & Baas, 1992) and echoing Hilden's demonstration that 20 randomly chosen samples drawn from a concourse of 1,500 items can produce the same factor structure (Hilden, 1958). This has led Brown to recently argue 'any Q sample that is representative of the concourse is just as good as any other' (Brown, 2012). De Graaf also notes that the sampling is a process of creating functional rather than logical clusters: 'The research does not logically construct the clusters. They result from the empirical data; they are operant' (2010, p. 8).

In a fourth example, the research design underpinning Cuppen's (2010) Q study is described in detail in earlier work (Cuppen et al., 2010) where Q is used to explore the range of ideas and opinions in the Netherlands surrounding the use of biomass. For Cuppen, concourse is defined as 'the full range of discussions and discourse on the particular issue under study. Defining concourse means identifying sources, either written or spoken, which contain ideas, opinions, values, preferences and knowledge claims on the issue under study' (Cuppen et al., 2010, p. 582). Here the authors report collecting over 200 statements from transcripts of discussion with those involved in a formal stakeholder dialogue in which the authors had been involved. They also drew statements from public debates, reports and newspaper articles. The authors suggest the mainstream media was an excellent source of statements expressing mainstream opinion and this was complemented by marginal views expressed in stakeholder transcripts. To create their Q set they suggest that 'these statements should reflect the diversity of the concourse. This set has to be reduced to a manageable number... while still reflecting the full diversity of viewpoints, claims and ideas'. The authors each individually categorised and identified unique statements within categories, and then compared, discussed and iteratively refined their categorisations until they reached an agreed Q set. Some 62 statements were piloted with five people to check for coherence and any omissions. A final Q set of 60 statements was retained.

In a fifth example (Jeffares & Skelcher, 2011), the researchers were interested in the democratic perspectives of public administrators and how this shapes their perception of working in governance networks. They drew on a combination of academic literature and interview transcripts from their own previous research. This produced around 300 statements. To sample, they employed a 3×3 matrix, modified from that of Dryzek and Berejikian (1993). The modified matrix sampled definitions, opinions prescriptions, relationships, degree of agency and motivation. In stripping out duplicates they also ensured a roughly equal balance across a previously published typology (Klijn & Skelcher, 2007). The final set consisted of 36 items.

The overall claim of the studies featured in Table 4.1 is that they are opening up the policy process, revealing tacit debates and enhancing participative democracy. They are showing us the structure of debates previously little understood. They are capable of considering vast and complex debates and giving them simple structures. They draw on a plethora of sources, from first hand interviews to media reports, published studies, transcripts and focus groups. Where voices are difficult to hear, we see a creative selection of sources.

In terms of representing the debate in a Q set, the studies vary in the degree to which they structure the sampling. They range from the iterative and deliberative process of Cuppen to the structured approaches of de Graaf and Ockwell. The studies assure us that it is ultimately respondents that give meaning and shape to these factors, that this is a functional rather than a logical exercise.

Having compared these studies in terms of how they assess, draw and sample policy concourse, it is now important to reflect on this practice. Below are three remarks concerning volume, time and transparency.

Volume

The first remark is in regard to volume. In each example above, the process of developing the Q set requires many hours of sifting through a range of sources.

Time

The second remark is in regard to time. The descriptions of how researchers sampled concourse made little or no mention of the temporal change of concourse during the period of enquiry. They were content to draw statements from a mixture of sources, both contemporary and historical. If the concourse was intended to be sensitive to change and fluctuation, this approach to capturing concourse made little acknowledgement of this.

Transparency

The third remark is about transparency. While it is possible to extract information about how the concourse was captured and sampled, what and how this is reported varies considerably across the literature. Seldom is it mentioned, for example, how or why a particular quote is identified, how sources are selected for review, what level of reading takes place, how potential statements are recorded, or how saturation of concourse is evaluated.

These remarks on volume, time and transparency are interlinked and grow in importance once we start to reflect on the task in hand. Aside from some forms of historical institutionalism, by and large, what distinguishes policy analysis from historical analysis is the here and now. For some it is 'speaking truth to power', or in some form engaged in the policy process. When Q methodology is assisting public policy research it needs to be possible to match fast-moving developments, to efficiently appropriate and credibly reflect the changing concourse of debate. In policy research the luxury of three years of collecting statements, six months of sampling and 75 in-depth interviews are usually only possible in PhD research or large-scale projects.

The Total Place study introduced earlier in the chapter is by no means a corrective. The concourse of statements was drawn from observations of meetings, interviews, media reports, blogs and related media. A total of 221 statements were sampled on a framework influenced by Newman

(2001), resulting in a total of 42 statements. The subsequent change of government that occurred shortly after the study was carried out revealed Total Place to be a short-lived policy idea. It became an example of how the gestation of the research from conception to analysis could be out of sync with the lifecycle of policy ideas.

Conclusion

This chapter started out by exploring how to map viewpoints surrounding policy ideas. The previous chapter had suggested the early months of a policy idea provided a foundation upon which additional demands and meanings could be placed. The chapter applied Q methodology to a policy idea of Total Place. The method involved capturing the diversity of the debate (concourse), sampling this into a set of statements (Q set) and administering this to policy actors using a card sorting process (Q sort). By asking every respondent to sort using the same instruction and standardised sorting grid, it was possible to correlate sorts, extract factors and produce idealised Q sorts from factor arrays. These idealised Q sorts were interpreted as shared viewpoints surrounding the policy idea. In the case of Total Place, four viewpoints were interpreted. Viewpoints were named, characterised, distinguished and illustrated by drawing on quotes from respondents whose own Q personal sort most closely resembled (and informed) a particular viewpoint.

By applying Q methodology to the understanding of policy ideas, the chapter also highlighted how policy actors are engaged in games of meaning. For emergent policy ideas, the label might be static, but the meaning is fluid. It reminds us that viewpoints do not belong to particular 'types of people' but rather these viewpoints emerge through a process of socialisation and exposure to information about the policy idea during early stages.

The final section of this chapter explored the challenge of approaching the concourse or volume of debate surrounding a policy idea. It argued that although Q methodology offers exciting possibilities for public policy research, the legitimacy of Q methodology hinges not on the representativeness of respondents (the person sample) but the ability of the researcher to capture and sample the concourse. The review of previous studies in the final section of this chapter highlighted volume, time and transparency as three challenges to capturing and sampling concourse in public policy studies using Q.

Policy studies using Q earnestly report a process of careful concourse interpretation, and close reading or exposure to debates through review, observation, interview or web search. However, in an era of new online communication and comment, where policy ideas are launched and discussed through social media platforms, the character of this process is high volume and high velocity. The next chapter will now explore the way in which policy is discussed on social media platforms and begin to consider the opportunities and challenges this offers for public policy research in an era of hashtag politics.

5

Social Media and Policy Practices

It would be all too easy to extol the merits and exaggerate the importance of social media for the policy process. This chapter casts a critical eye over such claims, focusing on the favoured platform of policy actors: Twitter. It explores the social media practices of policy actors and reviews peer-reviewed research. The chapter draws on a comprehensive review of published research to better understand how policy actors are engaging with social media. It illustrates emerging social media practices with a case study of a policy implemented in 2012 in England and Wales, to replace local appointed police authorities with directly elected PCCs.

This chapter reveals that although computational social science is beginning to capitalise on this 'social data revolution' (Hubbard, 2011), the literature shows a diversification in how social media data are used. The chapter has three sections. The first explores social media practices; the second explores commercial and democratic literatures from business studies and sociology; the third section reviews social media research in political science and literature of professional practice. It concludes that although plenty of research focuses on the social media campaigns of politicians, brand launches, social movements and fund-raising, there is relatively little on how policy ideas are implemented across social media.

Social media practices

To begin to understand the impact of social media on policy-making, this first section focuses on how policy actors use Twitter. It seeks to explore the messages, or 'Tweets' that policy actors exchange on Twitter; their motivation for doing so and implications for research. For readers who are long-established on Twitter this might read as something of a primer; for those readers it might be helpful to use this section to reflect on how and why they tweet about policy. This section is purposefully descriptive, offering a foundation to the second half of the chapter that surveys explanations of published research.

Established in 2006, Twitter is a website available all over the world that provides a platform for users to share 140-character messages. As public messages they are then searchable and available to anybody online, whether or not they are a user of Twitter. Users are able to 'follow' other users and can be alerted to new messages. When famous people or corporations join Twitter they can find themselves amassing followerships of thousands, sometimes millions of followers. Most active users, however, have closer to 100–200 followers made up of colleagues, friends and family. News organisations, bloggers, businesses and politicians find Twitter an effective means to disseminate messages and remain 'ambiently aware' (Kaplan & Haenlein, 2010). Each user has a unique Twitter ID, known as their 'handle' (such as @UKHomeOffice, @BarackObama). Although the limit is 140 characters, users are able to include hyperlinks to content on the internet such as pictures, looping videos, blogs, articles or websites. Furthermore the evolution of smart phone technology means linked material, such as links to photos or websites are displayed as photographs with captions.

There are three conventions that have emerged to enhance the spread of information on Twitter, depicted by the symbols @, RT, #. The first, @, or 'mention', is used when mentioning another user or replying to one of their messages. The message is directed at a specific user but readable and searchable to all. These can be either new messages or replies, allowing for conversation between users.

The second is RT, or retweet, which essentially involves a user discovering a message written by another user and forwarding it to their own followership in an unmodified form, meaning the message will appear to the followers of the user retweeting the message. The practice of retweeting means a message can spread virally through networks of followers within minutes of the original tweet.

Third is the # (the hash symbol or what some call the pound sign), known as the hashtag, which allows users to flag or tag their message as belonging to a current discussion or issue. A message tagged with a hashtag is added to a channel, a stream of content and easily searchable. Twitter's algorithms determine the most popular subjects on Twitter from moment to moment and help users discover trends. Although the first hashtags were used around 2007, they became widely used by users and organisations from around 2010 onwards and since then other platforms including Facebook, Google+, Tumblr and Pintrest have since adopted the hashtag to tag content for discussion and navigation. It is worth also noting that a second purpose of hashtags is to express sentiment or add inflection to comments. This will be discussed further below.

These practices have evolved in the first five years of Twitter and will continue to do so. The simplicity of the 140 character limit means that users can follow their most favoured and trusted people or organisations and have an up-to-the-second sense of what is happening and what others think. An example of a tweet from the PCC election campaign of November 2012 is as follows:

RT @PoliceElections: BREAKING: @UKHomeOffice #MyPCC site has had 1,000,000 hits. @PoliceElections http://t.co/uy1yG2Bi has had 10,700,000 hits. #JustSaying #PCCs

In this example, the author of the tweet is comparing the number of people visiting an unofficial blog compared with the official Home Office website. It is purposefully hashtagged three times to ensure that it is picked up in search and trend monitoring: #PCC was the tag most frequently used by authors discussing the PCC election; the #MyPCC tag was one started by the Home Office when launching the PCC elections; and #JustSaying, was at the time a popular tag where people boast or express an opinion topic and then soften it with #JustSaying. It contains a link to the popular blog. Through the use of the @ symbol, it is directed at both the author of the popular blog and the official Home Office Twitter account, again making it searchable and bringing the issue to the attention of both website owners. Importantly, it is a RT (retweet), so it is being forwarded by this user to their own followers. So although less than 140 characters, much can be included in the body of the tweet. In practice the most effective tweets are shorter and simpler than this, allowing space for others to modify or discuss.

The tweet in this example refers to the elections for local PCC in England and Wales in November 2012. The tweet is critical of the official government website and designed to promote a private alternative. It is one of around 46,000 tweets in circulation during the three week build-up to the election held on 15 November 2012.

It is possible to identify a range of reasons why some of the actors engaged in policy implementation might tweet. Table 5.1 includes a range of examples. It shows politicians receiving and responding to questions, cascading messages, expressing opinion with a widely adopted hashtag, and also messaging with a personally created hashtag. It shows examples of a government department receiving critical messages from citizens, cascading messages from citizens and other departments, and drawing on official hashtags to publicise information and mobilise action. The table includes an example of a think tank cascading positive endorsement of their website and using hashtags to publicise it.

Table 5.1 also includes examples of news organisations and journalists cascading links to their content and publicising upcoming broadcasts related to the popular theme. We find citizens asking questions of the department and politicians, cascading and endorsing the messages of other users, commenting on the policy, politicians or events. We find them using Twitter to campaign and as a means to consult and source

Table 5.1 Examples of policy actors tweeting

The politician (John Prescott)	
@	@earthyjules Morning Julie. Go to http[link]://t.co/qAlBopuM, put in your postcode and read your #pcc candidate statements
	In reply to @johnprescott. Do you know who the #mypcc candidates are for leeds please?
RT	RT @mypcclinks: @johnprescott been up since 6 working on #MyPCC http[link]
	RT @1ElephantsChild:.@johnprescott If I didn't follow you on Twitter I wouldn't have known anything about the PCC election.
#	Unbelievable! Coalition incompetence means #PCC ballots costing £350,000 will have to be shredded! http[link]
	Night everyone. Early start tomorrow. Good luck to all #PCC candidates. Even the ones who want to 'stop' me! LOL! #JP4PCC
The Department (The Home Office)	
@	@BarryCooper15 wrote:
	@ukhomeoffice not launching its site for #mypcc until the 26th is confusing people and turning off those who would otherwise engage.
	@Toxophile wrote:
	@ukhomeoffice how much did the TV adverts for #MyPCC cost you to make? How much are the elections costing, what problem are they addressing?
RT	RT @rahulrashid: #MyPCC should tackle hate crimes and hooligans RT @ukhomeoffice #MyPCC will focus on the things I care about. What will yours do? Vote on, Ä
#	2 days until police & crime commissioner elections. Make sure you have your say #MyPCC http[link]://t.co/HXxu0wzF

Table 5.1 (Continued)

	A Think Tank (Policy Exchange)
@	@TweetFaiza wrote:
	Hi @policy_Exchange have you seen @ncvys #PCC #youthcharter http[link]://t.co/wHkUkSEs we have over 40 sign ups now! #thinkyouth pls RT
#	1 week until the #PCC elections! Our http[link]://t.co/IoTiQp3D site for comparing the candidates has clocked up over 6,000 hours of browsing time
	The Media (BBC)
To @	@EvanHD re #PCC piece this am, you said will be interviewing reps from all major parties this week. What about the Indies?
	@bbcbreakfast @bbcnews @itvnews @skynews @BBCPolitics @bbcradio4today @bbc5live Time for all #PCC candidates to declare who is funding them!
RT	RT @BBCEngland: The #PCC elections take place in two days, find out about the candidates in your area on the BBC's special page
#	Election excitement mounts. Just 9 days to the #pcc votes. On #r4today at 0810, we talk to Theresa May
	#PCC may not capture the public imagination, but we reject any measure of democracy at our peril @guardian http[link]://t.co/Iy6WI1S1
	Citizens
@	@ukhomeoffice total absence of info from any candidate for TVP so far. #MyPCC #dotheywantmyvote?
	@StuartAndrewMP one single high profile individual with power is far better than a large number of unknowns. #PCC elections.
	@Jacqui4hantspcc Hi, as my Labour #PCC candidate what is your view on police role re domestic violence, rape, child abuse? Big q in 140
RT	RT @benjiflute: I think Theresa May just convinced me that #PCC's are pointless. Interesting. #r4today
#	I think Theresa May just convinced me that #PCC's are pointless. Interesting. #r4today
	If you want to stop privatisation of West Mids police, vote for Mike Rumble on Thurs. The only candidate fit for purpose. @MikeRumble1 #pcc
	What questions do you think we should ask @tony4gtrmcr about how he will address disability hate crime issues if he is elected #pcc

ideas for upcoming events. (We also found spam and phishing accounts trying to capitalise on the popular hashtag, with tweets phrased to encourage users to click on a link, typically starting with #PCC and then a phase such as 'I can't believe this is true' and a link.)

The examples of practices in Table 5.1 are summarised in Table 5.2. It shows how five types of policy actor are utilising Twitter to communicate their activities or opinions. The mention function (@) allows the platform to function as an open email exchange that is public, transparent and searchable. The RT function serves as a means to cascade messages but also show endorsement of the message. Importantly, the original author of the tweet is notified when somebody retweets their message. It serves as a means of showing admiration or could be interpreted as a means of building rapport or seeking favour. To counteract this suggestion, some users explicitly state in their profile biographies that 'retweets are not necessarily a sign of endorsement'. Finally, it seems the use of a hashtag is about bracketing discussion or seeking to start a new discussion. It is used to label events or products and it is used

Table 5.2 Summary of policy actors tweeting

	@	RT	#
Politician	Receiving Fielding Responding Answering	Spreading positive Spreading praise Spreading negativity about others	Labelling opinion Creating theme
Government department	Receiving questions and criticism	Sharing and spreading personal message Cascading corporate message or news Sharing validation	Reminding/ resurrecting
Think tank	Receiving ideas/tip offs	Sharing validating endorsement of product	Publicising product
Broadcast Media	Receiving suggestion for interview/ coverage	Sharing product	Publicising product Inviting discussion
Citizen	Posing questions	Sharing and endorsing view of others	Labelling events positively/negatively Mobilising action #pcc

to resurrect ongoing debates. The hashtag is a purposive act. Not all tweets contain hashtags, but those that do are the result of a deliberate act among the authors to link the content of the tweet with a new or ongoing discussion.

The PCC example gives some insight into the motivation for policy actors to tweet. Although the adoption of Twitter among policy actors is difficult to quantify, it has recently established itself as a mainstream communication platform. The number of active users and rate of traffic has increased exponentially since 2009 (Page, 2012), and it briefly enjoyed the status of being the eighth most popular website in the world in 2012 (Alexa, 2013). The reach of Twitter into the world of policy and politics is demonstrated by the presence of corporate Twitter accounts in all UK government departments, and in 2013 Twitter accounts are held by 409 of the sitting 650 MPs (almost 63%, including 78% of Liberal Democrats, 57% of Labour and 67% of Conservatives are reported to be on Twitter (TweetMinster, 2013). It is estimated that 95% of British local authorities have Twitter accounts and 80% are on Facebook (BDO, 2013). In May 2012 the UK Cabinet Office relaxed its policy about use of social media, including Twitter (Cabinet Office, 2012). The availability of web-enabled smart phones and improved mobile internet speeds make this an accessible and attractive means to connect, share, show off and remain aware of current events.

The rise of Twitter has caught public policy research on the hop. Despite the now taken-for-granted presence of this technology, we remain in a period of discovery, with ill-defined academic rules and norms (Smith et al., 2012) and a range of novel challenges around how best to harness this type of social data; researchers are described as working in something of a 'grey area' (Neuhaus & Webmoor, 2012). Like the introduction of communications technology in the past, the rise of Twitter can be compared to the telegraph, the radio or the internet (Arceneaux & Weiss, 2010): despite the challenges for research, it is also a period of excitement and growth that mirrors, albeit 2–3 years behind, the growth of Twitter itself.

The next section reports a comprehensive review of recent literature exploring empirical and methodological research into social media practices and analysis. The review concludes that exciting and pathbreaking methodological developments, largely driven by commercial and democratic interests, are of considerable utility to emerging research in how social media is shaping political and professional practice. However, where political application of social media is studied, there is a preoccupation with tasks like predicting election outcomes or exploring how politicians use the technology. It seems there remains a gap concerning the role of Twitter in the communication or implementation of policy ideas.

Reviewing commercial and democratic literatures

The following review is based on a search of indexed articles found on the Thomson Reuters Web of Social Science in November 2012. A total of 324 article titles and abstracts were selected for review and of these, 114 papers were found to be relevant to the focus of this chapter and are discussed below.

The simplest means to divide this literature would be into two camps: commercial and democratic. The first is driven by commercial interests – audience, consumer and market insight. Much of this discussion takes place across the internet in blogs, grey literature and media content that is widely available online, but is often tied into specific products for customer insight analytics, or social media monitoring, whereby companies can monitor the airwaves for damaging discussion of brands. The focus of academic research is on synthesising and defining the terrain (Kaplan & Haenlein, 2010) and on case studies of campaigns that successfully combine social media platforms into a valuable 'social media ecosystem' (Hanna et al., 2011; Kaplan & Haenlein, 2012). This literature is aware that the scale and speed of social media mean that companies have to get the branding right if they want to thrive in this new online environment (Barwise & Meehan, 2010).

The commercial literature suggests that firms must acknowledge and harness the power of two-way communication (Sreenivasan et al., 2012), arguing that companies that utilise two-way communications are duly rewarded with loyal customers who are willing to pay more (Culnan et al., 2010; Parent et al., 2011) and researchers find that dialogical interaction across social media reduces feelings of negativity towards brands (Wigley & Lewis, 2012). A central concern for the commercial literature is automated sentiment analysis. This presents complex linguistic challenges: a tweet that says something is 'thin' may be positive or negative depending on whether it is a review of a laptop or a hotel's sheets, just as the phrase 'go read the book' may have different connotations depending on whether it a review of a book or a review of a film (Bjørkelund et al., 2012). To that end, the literature is preoccupied with developing, testing and proving the robustness of automated sentiment meters (Thelwall et al., 2011, 2012). While companies like to be able to monitor brand performance, there is also the lure of being able to use Twitter to predict share prices (Bollen et al., 2011), predict box office revenues (Asur & Huberman, 2010) or elections (Tumasjan et al., 2011), although others question the foundation of such claims (Jungherr et al., 2012).

The commercial literature is also interested in profiling users, and in how certain messages spread virally through networks of followers. For example, some suggest three types of user: Mass Media, such as the BBC relaying major topics to the majority, Evangelists and opinion leaders such as politicians and celebrities who have the capacity to introduce minor topics to dispersed networks; and Grassroots users, with limited agency, making up 98% of users (Cha et al., 2012).

In the commercial literature there is also an interest in researching and understanding the motivation to join and to contribute to social media discussion (Muntinga et al., 2011). Reasons suggested include the need for personal gratification and camaraderie (Chen, 2011); a desire for information and, importantly, attention (Rui & Whinston, 2012); others suggest users are motivated by an interest in attaining an 'ambient awareness' of news and events, for the purposes of exhibitionism and opportunities for voyeurism (Kaplan & Haenlein, 2011).

The commercial literature tries to establish, for example, which messages are most likely to be retweeted (Malhotra et al., 2012), or how many connections a user can maintain (Goncalves et al., 2011). This work utilises a variety of methods to explore social media data; for example experiments to determine users' perceptions of a person based on whether their profile contains high or low degrees of interactivity (Lee & Shin, 2012). Others are interested in how we can measure the influence of users, with klout.com emerging as one of the most recognised indexes issuing users with Klout scores of 0–100 based on the influence of their activity on Twitter and other platforms (Serrano-Puche, 2012).

An alternative to the commercial literature discussed above is most succinctly described as 'democratic': that which highlights or questions the democratic potential of social media use. This democratic literature has been given prominence by high profile examples of revolutions in Tunisia and Egypt, known as the 'Arab Spring', and more recently social movements in Spain, Turkey, Moldova and Syria (Lotan et al., 2011; Mungiu-Pippidi & Munteanu, 2009; Papacharissi & Oliveira, 2012; Youmans & York, 2012) and social movements around events such as G20 meetings (Bratich, 2011).

A normative theme apparent through much of this literature promotes the potential of social media platforms as offering a space where a movement can organise and mobilise, speak a common language, agree on a definition of a situation and formulate a shared vision

(Lindgren & Lundstrom, 2011). Research is interested in the role of hashtags before and after critical events, such as the fall of Egypt's President Mubarak (Papacharissi & Oliveira, 2012), and in the democratising potential of Twitter as a platform that can operate on basic mobile phones with limited network connection (Bosch, 2012), making it popular in developing countries. In addition to a focus on events, there is also acknowledgement of the potential of Twitter to build communities (Gruzd et al., 2011), enabling local community awareness and connection to locality (Naaman et al., 2011).

Themes around the spread of ideas and influential individuals found in the commercial literatures are also present in the democratic literatures, albeit for different reasons. These literatures are interested in contagion, with a focus on information flows, and how issues can rapidly escalate (Lotan et al., 2011). In common with the commercial literatures, user types and roles are defined – such as the role of 'spreaders' who spread the message, aiding the process of social influence and complex contagion (Gonzalez-Bailon et al., 2011). But a key theme is a concern that in a situation where democratic activists are pitched against authoritarian regimes, the 'revenue seeking social media platforms' will usually favour the established regimes (Youmans & York, 2012). It is argued that the playing field is not as level as some might think, and that social media is dominated by celebrity and corporate users, where influence and dominance reflects off-line social economic hierarchies (Page, 2012) and gender division (Armstrong & Gao, 2011).

Although it appears that there is a disparate and shapeless population of 'i-reporters', 'policy tweeters' and 'commentators' capable of challenging the established elite, the continued presence of powerful intermediaries destabilises any radical experiments in democracy (Auer, 2011). Furthermore, although Twitter is a tool for both breaking news and democratic activism, in practice, most tweets simply relay information, while political dialogue is rare (Small, 2011).

Reviewing practice and political literatures

Although commercial and democratically focused papers dominate the literature, a fragmented raft of papers focuses on implications for a range of established practices across academia and practice. This is perhaps most clearly visible in journalism, in the use of Twitter as a resource for journalists for story ideas, scandals and sources (Lariscy et al., 2009; Waters et al., 2010); with discussion of how journalists use Twitter to develop personal brands (Bruns, 2012); their willingness to share information (Lasorsa et al., 2012); and how newspapers are adopting social media as a means to increase readership (Hong, 2012).

Social media also changes how TV and radio programmes engage their audiences, with the use of hashtags to create 'viewertariats' (Ampofo et al., 2011; Anstead & O'Loughlin, 2011), offering a platform for collective discussion of important socio-political issues (Norman, 2012).

Beyond the media, Twitter is said to have implications for other services and professions. In education research, Twitter is discussed as a tool for engaging students and increasing academic performance (Ebner et al., 2010; Junco et al., 2011). In healthcare, research suggests how social media can improve interaction between professionals and patients (Hawn, 2009) or promote smoking cessation (Prochaska et al., 2012), or how at times of crisis authorities can monitor social media (Sutton, 2009), and emergency management organisations can spread useful information, such as flood or earthquake warnings (Liu et al., 2012). It is reported that in the social sector, charities are using Twitter and Facebook to provide information, build a sense of community and promote action (Briones et al., 2011; Lovejoy & Saxton, 2012). The literature also identifies how charities, like other organisations, tend to use social media tools to broadcast rather than engage, and miss out on the potential for dialogue and community building (Waters & Jamal, 2011).

But engagement with social media brings challenges and potential problems too; for example, trusted public figures such as judges (Hull, 2012) or doctors (Greysen et al., 2010) have sometimes not understood the implications of what they say online. The volume and speed of activity and the large body of irrelevant personal messages and spam present challenges for those monitoring social media – this was highlighted as a problem during the outbreak of the H1N1 flu virus (Cheng et al., 2011). Furthermore, questions arise about when it is appropriate for public authorities to monitor what is said on Twitter, a practice that can be framed as either big brother-style intrusion and lurking, or, in a more positive light, 'social listening' (Crawford, 2009). While real-time information flows can assist the authorities in crises or criminal investigations, they can also serve to aid criminals, as in the case of the terrorist attacks in Mumbai in 2010 (Oh et al., 2011).

Writers argue that we are in an era of 'big data' (Boyd & Crawford, 2012; Mayer-Schönberger & Cukier 2013), where researchers from across science, mathematics, computing, arts and social science are 'clamouring' for massive quantities of information, in what is referred to by some as 'massified' research (Neuhaus & Webmoor, 2012), where online conversation is now searchable talk (Zappavigna, 2011). Datasets drawn from Twitter have grown exponentially with new methods of harvesting tweets – compare for example studies based on 653 tweets (Xifra & Grau, 2010) to half a billion(Efron, 2011; Wilkinson & Thelwall, 2012, not to mention the associated concerns around ethics and data management (Boyd & Crawford, 2012). But overall there is excitement in the literature around the potential of discovering, collaborating and disseminating research (Rowlands et al., 2011; Torres-Salinas & Delgado-Lopez-Cozar, 2009) and in the opportunities for specific disciplines, from medical research to international relations (Carpenter & Drezner, 2010).

Emerging from the political and policy sciences, a fourth grouping of Twitter literature comes from those involved in the scientific study of elections. Psephologists are interested in the role of Twitter in electoral performance (Tumasjan et al., 2011) and patterns of activity on Twitter during and after elections (Larsson & Moe, 2012). Elsewhere in political science there is a focus on why politicians are adopting Twitter (Chi & Yang, 2011; Lassen & Brown, 2011), how they are using Twitter for self-promotion (Golbeck et al., 2010), for communication with party colleagues (Hsu & Park, 2012), how it is being used during elections (Baxter et al., 2011), and comparisons of how national leaders tweet (Aharony, 2012).

As with the commercial literature, there is a theme in this political literature about political leaders not fully acknowledging the power of interaction (Grant et al., 2010). Some research has attempted experiments to 'prove' that marginal voters are more likely to favour a political candidate who uses their Twitter account for interaction. The potential of Twitter to develop what some are calling the 'micro-celebrity' (Marwick & Boyd, 2011) attracts both current and aspiring politicians who crave attention (Rui & Whinston, 2012), using the same means and techniques as sport and music stars (Hutchins, 2011).

Like companies, parties and politicians are subject to media events that can destabilise reputations and we see a focus in the literature on the role of Twitter in constructing and contesting events such as 'Bullygate', when the then British Prime Minister Gordon Brown was accused of bullying his staff (Chadwick, 2011).

The practice of hashtagging leads researchers naturally to track the fate of themes and ideas over days and hours rather than years, and to analyse the 'micro-dynamics' of an event. This is demonstrated clearly in the case of natural disasters (Friedman, 2011), such as the earthquakes in Fukushima (Binder, 2012) or Haiti (Smith, 2010), and political scandals (Chadwick, 2011). With the 2012 US election where the presidential candidates spent considerable resources on social media, including Twitter, research is interested in quantifying the value of such campaigns. Others have focused on audiences during candidate debates (Baxter et al., 2011) or on following notable policy decisions, such as the aftermath of Norway's decision to sign a European directive (Moe, 2012).

Four imperatives to research social media

Divided in this way, the emerging literature on social media in social science can be plotted as follows in Table 5.3: 1. Democratic, 2. Political, 3. Practice, 4. Commercial. The majority of the content is found in commercial and democratic literatures. The commercial literature is the best resourced and perhaps most innovative, but is also surrounded in commercial sensitivity, meaning much of the most exciting work takes place beyond the gaze of peer review behind commercial sensitivities and paywalls. The practice literature is most fragmented, divided by discipline and sector, but with a common motivation around how technologies such as Twitter will change practices in the media, public services and research communities. The political literature draws on a similar pool of

Table 5.3   Four motives of the Twitter literature(s)

1. Democratic	2. Political
Uprising, mobilisation, organise, democratic, accessible, events, local, community, contagion, escalation, off-line hierarchies, breaking news	Electoral performance, predicting results, politician adoption, self-promotion, broadcasting, micro-celebrity, events/disasters, micro-dynamics, social media campaigns
Enthusiast seeking foundation	Rigorous and narrowly focused
3. Practice	**4. Commercial**
Journalist resource, broadcast viewertariats, student and patient, donor engagement, issue of disclosure, volume and speed, crisis management, intelligence, big brother, listening	Campaigns, branding, dialogue, sentiment, robust, automated, prediction, monitor, Klout, influence, user types, return on investment, behaviour change
Massified research, big data, ethics and data management	Methodologically advanced but opaque
Curious but fragmented	

methods and statistical modelling but is narrowly focused on elections and party politics (Table 5.3).

Plotting it in this way, however, masks the differing levels of maturity and coherence of these literatures. The commercial interests associated with understanding the power of Twitter will continue to drive business schools. Furthermore, the democratic potential and the rich and high profile case studies of recent years will drive the work of sociologists engaged in the democratic literature. The impact on practice will vary across disciplines as educators, researchers, police, medics and journalists develop rules and norms about how to engage with this technology.

A central concern resulting from this review is the question of *where next* for the political sphere. As it stands, the psephologists are advancing with their study elections with twitter data, and political scientists more generally are increasingly interested in how politicians are engaging with this relatively new tool on their mobile telephones, and where there are opportunities for Twitter to map the micro-dynamics of political events.

In an attempt to further explore the role Twitter for public policy analysis, it is possible to imagine the role of Twitter in terms of a policy cycle of problem identification, possible solutions, selection, decision, implementation and review. Plotting the use of Twitter in this way highlights its contribution to public policy, while also revealing gaps in our knowledge. Expressed in terms of a policy cycle:

- Problem identification – Twitter can amplify or communicate a problem requiring policy redress. Policy-makers may be alerted by their own followers or use social media monitoring software to identify issues that require attention.
- Range of solutions – potential solutions directed at the problem – perhaps identified with a hashtag – can be found in a body of tweets.
- Selection of solution – a proposed way forward can be discussed and an issue put out to consultation. It is possible for policy-makers to collect the discussion on Twitter around an issue and use it to inform their decision.
- Implementation of policy solution – Twitter can be used as a device to spread the message about an event, a process, or a piece of information to help in the implementation of the policy. This could be a corporate Twitter account belonging to the responsible department making regular policy announcements and updates. Precedents can be found in fund-raising and election campaigns.

- Evaluation/review – Twitter could be used to formally or informally capture a range of views on the issue, interim reports, formal assessment and review.

The role of social media in helping to reveal and communicate a situation as a policy problem requiring attention is a key consideration for all four of the literatures identified above. For the commercial literature it is a question of brand and reputation; for the political and practice literatures, perhaps a natural disaster requiring attention; and for the democratic literature the successful mobilisation of activists using social media.

In terms of discussing and selecting a solution, the potential is primarily consultative. For advocates, it is about crowdsourcing solutions, and an opportunity to test responses to an outline proposal. Similarly, regarding evaluation and review, interim reports, the outcome, the process of evaluation or review can all make use of social media.

It is the fourth aspect of this process – the implementation of policy – that is neglected in the literature. A rare exception is Moe's 2012 case of Norway's decision to ratify the European Data Directive (2012). His study includes some 4,500 tweets discussing the decision over a six-month period. Advocates of the democratic potential of Twitter suggest that it offers a means to destabilise the implementation of public policy. However, in the case of Norway, the majority of tweets came from just a handful of policy actors, and the discussion lost momentum. Why and how this happened is not clear, and important questions for further research are raised. It is important not to neglect the implementation of policy through Twitter. We are now in an era where government departments across the world are maintaining corporate Twitter accounts. As discussed above, themes emerging across the different spheres of literature include the implications for dialogue, loyalty, reduced negativity, building communities, promoting action and conversing (Parent et al., 2011; Briones et al., 2011; Culnan et al., 2010; Lovejoy & Saxton, 2012; Sreenivasan et al., 2012; Wigley & Lewis, 2012).

Combined with a social media ecosystem including YouTube and Facebook, there is potential for an effective implementation of policy, be it maintaining a policy idea such as the Big Society or implementing a seasonal road safety campaign.

But we can also see from experience in other sectors that where corporate tweeting is implemented, it tends to focus on broadcasting rather than interaction. Examples in the literature of corporate tweeting include a study of 200 charities all using Twitter but with a tendency for using their Twitter feed for one-way dissemination of information (Waters & Jamal, 2011); an example of 488 local US TV stations using their accounts to announce news stories (Greer & Ferguson, 2011); an example of South Korea's Ministry of Agriculture focusing mainly on one-way communication and risk management (Cho & Park, 2012); an example of three airlines mainly tweeting marketing messages, with most public tweets coming from customers with complaints, to which the company could have publicly replied, but did not.

Research that reports the content of tweets is essential in determining whether messages are cascaded through the practice of retweeting. Creating a social media ecosystem is not always easy when your reputation is damaged, as BP found when trying to use social media to rebuild their reputation following the Gulf Coast oil spill (Muralidharan et al., 2011). There is always potential for certain types of users, particularly 'spreaders' and 'evangelists', to use their influence to spread potentially destructive themes, often through 'hashtag crashing'.

By creating hashtags, they are creating the public policy equivalent of the viewertariats, as used by TV programmes. The creation of policy hashtags is therefore the creation of 'policytariats', interconnected communities free to express their views about the policy, in which the creators might well be unable to manage the consequences of critique or derision or where policy actors lack the expertise or tools to monitor sentiment or distinguish discussion among masses of irrelevant messages and spam. But judging by the growth in use of Twitter among government departments and politicians, it seems many see more benefits than pitfalls.

Conclusion

This chapter has explored how social media platforms are providing a means for people to express and share information and opinion using computers, phones and other wireless devices. The example from the PCC election showed how in a policy context policy actors use Twitter in a variety of ways for communicating, cascading and labelling content. The chapter reported published social science research located in four literatures, each with their own motivations to understand the growth in social media use. The democratic literature focuses on events, mobilisation and problem definition. The political literature is concerned with impact on politics and elections. The commercial literature seeks to understand impact and role of social media in prediction. Practice oriented literatures argue that social media is reshaping the practices of a wide variety of professions, from journalists to police, and from academics to medics.

Policy actors might have been relatively late to the party, but Twitter, like Facebook and YouTube, has emerged as a platform to launch and foster policy initiatives. But this raises questions. Does implementing a policy initiative equate to implementing a social media campaign for a new brand of coffee, a fund-raising campaign for a charity or the election campaign of a political party? This chapter has argued that the use of social media platforms by policy actors remains little understood. While policy actors have support from communications staff, PR agencies and campaign managers, what use are their tools and techniques in terms of launching and maintaining policy initiatives? By and large, public policy research is relatively silent on this.

Social media analytics has grown rapidly in recent years out of a need to predict markets, elections or social unrest. Others remain excited by the democratic potential of mobilisation and education. This chapter has moved the debate on to focus on the potential of social media data as both a mechanism for communicating and analysing policy ideas. The next chapter explores how this might work in practice.

6
Capturing the Digital Footprint of Policy Discussion

In 2013 there were, on average, 4,600 new tweets and 11,500 new Facebook posts made every second. There are two possible approaches to understanding and analysing this global activity: 'monitor and visualise', or 'capture and sift'. This chapter explores both. This chapter explores how to monitor, visualise and capture this voluminous, uncategorised stream of data. The chapter is divided into two sections: the first section explores the role and potential of tools designed to monitor and visualise social media activity. The second section explores how it is possible for researchers to capture data from social media platform APIs (Application Programming Interfaces) for the purposes of analysis. The chapter is illustrated through a case study of the official hashtag of the 2012 Police and Crime Commissioner election: #MyPCC. The chapter finds that monitor and visualise tools offer real-time visualisation of the changing dynamics of discussion of policy ideas, but that only by capturing their own data can researchers attain a richer and interpretive understanding of this stream of data.

Monitor and visualise

Ignorance of what is occurring or is being said can be detrimental to reputation, as is encapsulated by the resignation of the BBC's Director General in November 2012, who had been in the job for just 54 days. The antagonistic radio interview on the morning of his resignation captures well the challenge:

> Interviewer (John Humphrys): But you must have known what happened – a tweet was put out 24 hours beforehand, 12 hours beforehand, telling the world that something was going to happen

on Newsnight that night that would reveal extraordinary things about child abuse and that would involve a senior Tory figure from the Thatcher years, you didn't see that tweet?

George Entwistle: I didn't see that tweet John, I now understand…

I: Why not?

GE: I check Twitter sometimes at the end of the day sometimes – or I don't check Twitter at all…

I: …You have a staff! But you have an enormous staff of people who are reporting into you on all sorts of things – they didn't see this tweet that was going to set the world on fire?

GE: John, this tweet I'm afraid was not brought to my attention so I found out about this film after it had gone out. (Transcribed from BBC Radio 4 interview, 10 November 2012)

As Chapter 5 reported, there are several imperatives to monitor social media activity. The review of the commercial literature in the previous chapter highlighted the importance of monitoring sentiment towards a brand, a commercial imperative to measure fluctuation in brand sentiment. The political imperative focuses around campaigns – is Romney outperforming Obama in the social media sphere in the run up the election? Can we track social media sentiment against polling data? Can we predict the outcome of elections? The democratic imperative concerns which issues are important and where, what hashtags are contagious, or 'trending', and how are they being used? Who are the influencers in this discussion?

The professional imperatives vary across sectors. For journalists, for example, they could include monitoring which stories are big and gaining insights into stories from the discussion online. The imperatives are both informational and economic. Public organisations are investing in social media technology to 'channel shift' frontline communication with citizens away from what are considered 'expensive' interactions such as phone calls or face-to-face interviews (Paul Dale, 2012). Government agencies are required to respond to crises, bomb threats, natural disasters and riots. Emergency agencies can cascade information and help to manage the emergency. But agencies also want to know if there is a change in mood, or a form of backlash towards the administration, the policy or the campaign. They are interested in who the influencers are, who is trusted and influential, who they should beware of or who they should seek to align with.

What these imperatives in Table 6.1 share is a need for a real-time sense of what is happening online. While the providers of social media

Table 6.1   Four imperatives for using social media and examples of policy actors

Democratic	Political
Hashtag use by country/city/type	Election graphs
Sociologists, ethnographers	Political scientists
	Pollsters
	Sabermetricians
Practice	**Commercial**
Current issues (journalists)	Brand discussions
Drug discussion (Public Health)	e.g. Movie reviews
Criminologists	Sentiment
Police	Business intelligence analysts
Fraud investigators	Market researchers
Lawyers	
Journalists	
Historians	
Librarians	

platforms increasingly offer means to visualise, just as Google Trends reveals search preferences of Google users (Choi & Varian, 2012), the arrival of social platforms heralded something of a Gold rush to provide social media monitoring tools to the industry. This field, characterised by Silicon Valley start-ups, by the start of 2012 was undergoing a period of consolidation, merger and acquisition. The early market leaders were Radian6, Attensity, OpenAmplify, SAS Sentiment Analysis, Sysmos, Ohmygov, Clarabridge, Topsy, Datasift and Adobe Social. Alongside these, established consumer insight companies such as TNS, G&K, IPsos MORI, Mintel, Cello, insight Research Group, SPA Future Thinking, CIE group and ICM were establishing social media consumer insight units to run alongside their more conventional teams of pollsters, customer panels and focus groups. Monitoring social media had become big business. These companies and tools seek to make sense of unstructured data, or big data, for a variety of purposes. The analogy here is listening – social listening, active listening – they seek to listen to what has become known as the 'voice of the consumer'.

For example, one company, Crowdverb, offered the Complete Signal Analysis tool, powered by 'behavior metrics', which is about knowing your audience and knowing their preferences. Like news of the stock market, their media sentiment index shows, for example, how overall trust in Fox News can be up one percentage point to 47%, and trust in TV host Jon Stewart can be down four percentage points on the previous day. This is the kind of promise these websites and tools offer large organisations:

> Belief, confidence, credibility, and reliability are factors upon which trust is built ... or broken; this is true for brands, candidates, companies, movements, or products.... With Crowdverb, you can immediately begin building statistically relevant information; we give you a method to understand the audience or the market that is automated, easy to understand, and frankly – simple to use. If you can identify the audience, we can deliver the data you need to understand and manage trust. Not only can we help you gauge and understand current perspective, we give you the ability to build a reliable strategy to gain, increase, and solidify trust. Trust can be fragile and prone to change; Crowdverb keeps you attuned and ahead of the curve.
>
> (Crowdverb, 2012)

Many of the tools and companies listed above offer paid monthly or yearly subscriptions. In its simplest form users employ tools like HootSuite or Buffer to tweet from multiple accounts or track particular hashtags. One of the main offers of some of the paid subscription services is to offer organisations a tool that would flag up potential problems and alert the person best suited to respond. Where companies are offering real-time sentiment monitors they do so by cross-checking with hundreds of billions of tweets and posts indexed in their databases. As the industry matures it is in danger of becoming a battle of who has the biggest database.

One of the key markets for these monitor and visualise companies is local and national government. In May 2012 in the UK the department overseeing the running of the civil service, the Cabinet Office, issued guidance suggesting that departments should use social media corporately, and should maintain these social media accounts through a 'mediation service' to allow for 'greater monitoring and control' of social media websites, and manage who has the login credentials to post on corporate accounts (Cabinet Office, 2012). They suggested that these mediation services be included as part of a 'wider social media monitoring package'. The guidance outlined three kinds of risks and costs that should be considered when selecting a provider: consideration of the set up and running costs; ensuring the software is sufficiently 'useable' to be the preferred means of interacting/posting/tweeting; and preserving the freedom to move data to a new supplier if need be. As a case study they highlight how the Department for Work & Pensions

(DWP) had been exploring the potential of 'social media dashboard monitoring' to manage and coordinate communication of campaigns, to monitor activity and evaluate effectiveness. The DWP was highlighted as an example of best practice in how it used social media to publicise grants and evaluate impact (Department of Work & Pensions, 2012).

The transcript of the interview with the BBC Director General above is an extreme but telling example of why public organisations need to be continuously aware of what is being said about them and their campaigns. The example suggests that making policy in this environment requires the capability to listen. The volume of activity surrounding a policy also poses a challenge for analysis. The next section explores what *monitor and visualise* software can reveal about the discussion of policy on social media platforms.

Example part 1: Visualising #MyPCC

In this section a subscription-based *monitor and visualise* tool called Topsy Pro was used to study how the Home Office used social media when implementing the first national elections for local PCCs. It is worth noting here that there are an ever-growing range of tools available; Topsy Pro was chosen as it seemed to offer a comprehensive range of measures. It is also worth flagging here the fluid and rapidly growing state of the online analytics industry at the time of enquiry, and the difficulty of using such tools for rigorous scientific enquiry. In their defence, however, what they do offer is a means to rapidly assess current activity and, in some cases, provide an historical record.

In the Autumn of 2012, the Home Office was the department responsible for implementing the elections of PCCs in 41 local areas in England and Wales. Initially a manifesto pledge in 2010, the idea was that this new high profile position would replace the current appointed police authorities and improve local accountability in the police. Social media had been elevated as a primary means to inform the electorate about this election, as the government had rejected proposals to fund candidate mailshots; instead candidates were advised to embrace blogs, websites, Twitter, YouTube and Facebook to publicise their campaigns.

The Home Office launched its own social media campaign using a YouTube advertisement that was also shown on TV, and related tweets were tagged consistently with #MyPCC. Using Topsy Pro to search for #MyPCC, it was possible to visualise the activity, in terms of how many tweets were sent per day. Reminiscent of the 'policy as activity' measures

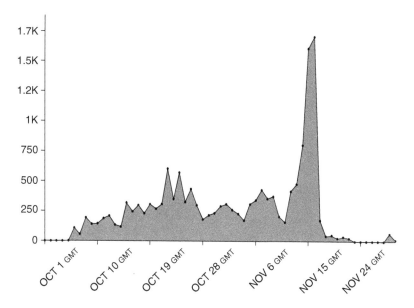

Figure 6.1   Mentions of #MyPCC on Twitter October–November 2013
Source: Topsy.com.

in Chapter 3, Figure 6.1 shows the fluctuation of tweets mentioning #MyPCC.

Before all else it should be noted that #MyPCC was the 'official' policy hashtag coined by the Home Office to be used across their social media campaign. They encouraged others to adopt it when discussing the PCC election. The majority of tweets related to the election did not use this hashtag, but favoured a shorter hashtag #PCC instead. The daily activity of #MyPCC tweets varied between around 150 and 600 per day in the build-up to the election, peaking at 1,700 on the day of the election.

Regarding the build-up to the election, depicted in Figure 6.1, the first spike of note is when the prime minister tweeted his support for the election (22nd October, 635 tweets). Contrast this with a dip on the 5th November – 174 tweets and no notable Home Office activity. With a week to go before the election the Home Office tweeted again and this led to 24 tweets from the Home Office, and 431 overall. Again on the 11th November the Home Office tweeted again – 4 days to go – 'They will hold your police force to account'. This generated 22 new tweets but a dip in the overall number back down to 161 tweets. It then increased on the 13th, 14th and 15th, doubling each day – and then a slight rise to peak on the 16th – the day of the results. Top tweets on the day of the election (the 15th) were the Home Office – tweeting at 7am – 'Polling stations across England and Wales have now opened for the Police and Crime Commissioner Elections' – 76 tweets – along with similar tweets at 1pm, 9pm and 10pm. On results day (the 16th) the top tweets were the PM and Home Office with late morning tweets to say that the results were expected later in the day. By the 17th the activity was mopping up the final results from Devon and Cornwall. By the 23rd November the use of #MyPCC was recorded as zero.

For an issue of considerably greater velocity and volume, such as the election of a new US president or appointment of a new pope, it might be necessary to focus on hours rather than days. However, Figure 6.1 gives us an initial sense of how Twitter was used day by day during the election period. It suggests that much of the activity was condensed into just a few days and that activity fluctuated during the build-up.

To get a sense of why certain days led to greater activity, it is desirable to explore the terms that were most related to the campaign. The list of the top related terms included: police commissioners, November, criminals, polling stations, Leicestershire, #police.

We might also be interested in the people who were associated with the MyPCC hashtag. Topsy offer an option to discover the 'Experts' – their definition of the most influential users related to the hashtag. This is a measure of who mentions the term the most along with a consideration of their influence. This is calculated in part by a focus on the number of followers of a user, but also in terms of whether their discussion of MyPCC was forwarded by others. In this case the top Experts were listed as, perhaps unsurprisingly, the Home Office (97 tweets, 91 retweets and a Topsy influence score of 5/5), and @dietjustice (31 tweets, 20 retweets, influence score of 2/5). The rest of the list had not engaged with the hashtag in any notable way. What can we tell from this? Perhaps that #MyPCC was very much a Home Office campaign idea. A policy actor can suggest a hashtag for everybody to use, but this does not necessarily mean it will be adopted. It suggests that #MyPCC did not catch on or develop as an organic concept.

Rather than focus on people or associated words, an alternative is to focus on the performance of particular tweets. An implicit concern of this kind of work is whether certain tweets have the capacity to reshape the trajectory or subjectivity of a policy idea. The first thing to look for would be to rank order the tweets in terms of influence – how many times were they retweeted by others and when did such a tweet peak? Such analysis might reveal that there was one solitary game-changing tweet that took the campaign in a different direction, but I would argue that this is rarely the case. Instead this analysis suggests that, over the course of the lifecycle of a policy idea, high performing tweets can be recorded but they will have influence in different spheres and follower networks. In the case of the PCC election, of the two 'top' MyPCC tweets for the duration of the campaign, one came from the BBC and another from the Home Office, offered in the early stages of the campaign: '*#MyPCC will focus on things I care about. What will yours do?*'

The focus on a single tweet also allows us to think of the lifecycle of a tweet. Such focus tells us immediately that, like mayflies, tweets seldom live beyond a single day. The example shows that, in its first morning of life, the tweet above was retweeted by 58 others. Further Topsy metrics show that it was only tweeted five times by 'Influential' users. It is reported to have a momentum score of 51 and an acceleration of −10. The only thing that does have a longer lifespan than a tweet is the link itself. A link to a blog or a site may be used several times at different stages of a campaign (Figure 6.2).

While the activity measure of tweets (Figure 6.1) is a measure of how many tweets were made during the MyPCC campaign, what also matters is how many people actually saw those tweets. It could have been possible that all of the tweets in Figure 6.1 came from one user feed, and that person had no followers; in this case, page impressions would be negligible. So it is important to consider how many page impressions, or how many times the MyPCC tweets appeared in users' personalised feeds (known as 'timelines').

Figure 6.3 shows that the first peak came on 15 October 2012, following the BBC's article 'Social Media and the PCC Elections: Tweeting

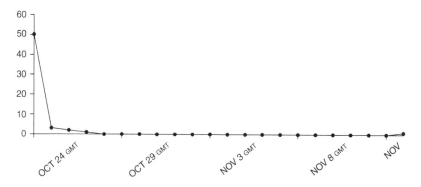

Figure 6.2   The 24-hour life of a tweet
Source: Topsy.com.

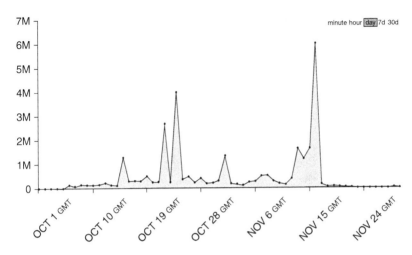

Figure 6.3 Fluctuations in page impressions of #MyPCC October–November 2012 on Twitter

Source: Topsy.com.

candidates' (Kasprzak, 2012). This article achieved 1.2m page or feed impressions. The next peak occurred on the 22nd October when the Prime Minister, David Cameron, tweeted about the election, and this was retweeted 35 times, contributing to the 2.6m impressions that day. The next peak, four million impressions, came on the day of the deadline for candidates to register, led by BBC and Home Office activity. Figure 6.3 shows how the number of daily impressions then dropped off, with daily exposure in the low hundreds of thousands. There was a brief resurgence over the next few days, with reminders from the Home Office that there were 'two weeks to go', amounting to 1.3 million impressions, which then dropped off again. The next time impressions exceeded one million was 13th November, when both the BBC and Home Office started sharing information about the candidates and how to vote. The resurgence was also buoyed by a tweet where a user decided to share an email exchange with a candidate. This tweet achieved twice the impressions of the Home Office reminder that day. It was not sufficient to derail the policy, but it added to a broader and cumulative sense of negativity during the build-up to the election.

The tweeting during the day of the election itself saw an exponential rise in page impressions, to a peak of six million; this can be cross-referenced with Figure 6.1, showing activity that day peaking at around 1,700 tweets. This reinforces how activity can be condensed into a single day. The following day the page impressions dropped off dramatically from around six million to 156,000. And by 23rd November, no page impressions were reported. On 23rd November, one week after the result of the election, nobody tweeted using the MyPCC hashtag.

So far the focus of this analysis has been on frequencies and metrics, but what of mood, sentiment, opinion and attitude? This is what commercial brand managers are particularly keen on understanding in terms of the ability to monitor fluctuations in positivity and negativity. For the #MyPCC case, Topsy offers two visualisations. The first is to track positive and negative tweets. The main graphic on Figure 6.4 shows the frequency of tweets, with one line showing the negative and another showing the positive. Additionally the lower graphic shows fluctuations in the difference between positive and negative sentiment. The first observation to note here is the negative sentiment outweighing the positive. And second is the growth in the gap between positive and negative on the day of the election itself, suggesting that once mainstream attention grew around the policy, the positive tweets could not keep pace with negative tweets featuring #MyPCC.

However these arguments start to unravel when we begin to probe further to investigate the top positive and negative tweets on each day. For example, on 6th October the top 'negative tweet' was one from the Home Office informing TV viewers to watch out for the new PCC advertisement. This is a statement of information rather than the expression of an opinion, but the classifier codes this as a negative tweet. This raises questions about this type of broad sentiment monitoring: what

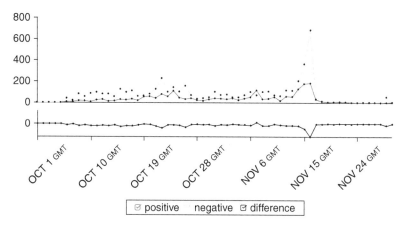

Figure 6.4 #MyPCC tweets: positive and negative
Source: Topsy.com.

is included and how? While the graphic seems plausible and seductively attractive to brand managers and those with a political or economic stake, it is difficult to validate.

In addition to tracking positive/negative tweets, the example tool offers a sentiment score, measured on a scale of 0–100, with 50 as neutral. Figure 6.5 shows the fluctuation of sentiment of MyPCC, revealing, for example, a surge in positive sentiment on the 3rd November, up 43 points. Such a graph is reminiscent of stock market performance or political polling, but it has to be interpreted with caution. The scores are standardised and do not reflect fluctuations in tweets from one day to the next. It also does not count every tweet, but only those considered to be expressing sentiment. For example, on one particular day, 15,441 tweets using #MyPCC were recorded, with 2,064 as positive in sentiment and 4,713 as negative, equating to a sentiment score of 31. Figure 6.5 shows that until the end of October the overall sentiment was negative, with a few peaks, such as one on the 6th November, followed by a drop of 57 points on the 8th November.

This prompts us to look for an explanation for this shift in sentiment in early November. The top tweet by far that day was a candidate tweeting 'No privatisation of Kent police' as a slogan. Do the terms 'no' and 'privatisation' suggest to the sentiment meter a rise of negativity? The example tweet was supportive of the elections: it was encouraging people to vote and to vote independent, and yet this tweet might have generated a reduction in sentiment towards the PCC election. Another point of caution should be in how we interpret the peak of sentiment on the 17th November, when the index hit 74. This could be seen as good news for the campaign, but it should be grounded by saying that it is based on just 39 tweets expressing opinion or sentiment that day,

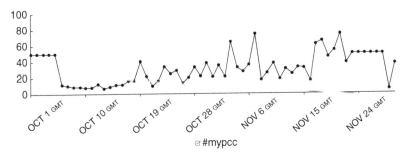

Figure 6.5 Example of an automated sentiment meter, #MyPCC
Source: Topsy.com.

somewhat less than the 1,718 opinionated tweets indexed on the 15th November. This example reveals something of the limitations of sentiment meters, as to whether they mask more than they reveal, and how to interpret scores.

To summarise this exploration of a 'monitor and visualise' tool, in this instance the sentiment analysis is rather opaque and does not reveal whether this is sentiment directed to the policy, the organisers, the candidates, or a specific candidate.

That said, the power of being able to historically track an issue in this way is potentially valuable. It is possible to identify key peak periods when a policy idea is most discussed – it is then possible to drill down and focus on key events. Furthermore it is also possible to focus not just on the volume of tweets, but the volume of page impressions. It is possible to identify key people or certain events that might have helped to introduce a theme about the policy to a wider audience.

It is important to restate at this point that MyPCC was not the most widely used hashtag for discussion of the PCC elections; the most popular was #PCC. The ratio of #MyPCC and #PCC was 1:15. Despite the PCC hashtag being adopted early by those tweeting about the election, the Home Office persevered, perhaps in ignorance, perhaps in hope, perhaps tenacity, with #MyPCC. To put it into context, Figure 6.6 shows the difference in page impressions between the two tags. The figure shows just English tweets, as the PCC hashtag was used in Indonesia and Brazil during this time in relation to other content.

If there is one thing that this brings into focus, it is the danger of conducting research by hashtag: choosing the wrong hashtag leads to poor recall (see also Kim, 2013).

The example in Figure 6.6 suggests that, despite being used by the Home Office and the BCC, the MyPCC hashtag did not gather momentum. To focus on just the official #MyPCC would be to overlook the vast majority of tweets related to the election.

Despite the potential of being able to monitor and visualise particular campaigns, hashtags or brands, there are limitations for public policy research once it comes to understanding sentiment. Automated sentiment meters might claim to be able to differentiate between angry birds and Angry Birds (derogatory descriptions of young women versus a popular video game franchise) but it seems they remain less attuned to a specific nationally or locally bounded policy idea unfolding online. The next section will explore some alternatives to monitoring and visualising social media activity that offer additional insights.

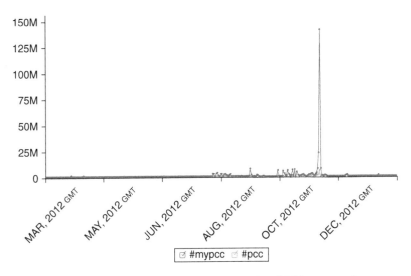

Figure 6.6 Comparing page impressions of MyPCC and PCC compared
Source: Topsy.com.

Capture and sift

Not all analysis of social media needs to be carried out in 'real-time'. The alternative to 'monitor and visualise' is to 'capture and sift', which entails setting up processes to capture social media streams for the purposes of analysis. In the early years of this kind of work, the only policy researchers able to capture data were those with programming skills. With the growth of social media platforms, applications and services began to appear. For instance, one application called Twapperkeeper was one of the first to offer this service to those interested in capturing tweets. Users would put in a request for all future tweets on a particular topic to be stored for later download. The researcher could then download the tweets as a file. The file would include additional metadata, such as date and user. Similar services have come and gone, but the trend is towards improved access to the full transaction of posts, with ever more metadata. However, these services come at a cost. By 2012 users were paying a few hundred US dollars per million units of social media data, with a full set of metadata, including Klout scores and so on. In contrast to 'monitor and visualise', the keywords associated with 'capture and sift' research include less appealing phrases: rather than 'listening', it is about 'scraping' sites; trawling, recording and harvesting content for later analysis.

The legitimacy of a 'capture and sift' application is judged by its interface with social media platforms. The interface between the application and the platform is accessed through an API. The proportion of the total feed that can be captured varies between platforms and arrangements. As platforms like Twitter and Facebook have grown in size, they have found it possible to limit access to their APIs or, notably, to monetise it. The size of archives is growing, with researchers capturing several million items on their chosen topic. Bearing in mind that a single post to a social media platform can include between 10 and 50 items of metadata, researchers that choose to 'capture and sift' are acquiring and attempting to make sense of increasingly massified datasets (Neuhaus & Webmoor, 2012). With the potential to capture everything comes a fear of missing out. With a full transaction rather than a sample of the conversation in the offering, there is a pressure on 'capture and sift' researchers to capture more, to miss nothing.

The review of the literature in Chapter 5 offered a brief but systematic introduction to what is a burgeoning and growing set of literatures interested in social media data. Where the approach of this book differs is in its interest in the content of the actual data, over and above the metadata. That is, much analysis of social media data reports, correlates and maps metadata; the data about the data, such as location, username and device type. For example, social network analysts use metadata to display social network relationships between posts that cross-reference one another. This can be seen in the increasingly elaborate and impressive aerial maps of who tweets during an event or how to spot the most affluent parts of a city by phone type and activity. If more than 5% of users regularly turned on location services on their devices, such maps would be even more detailed. Metadata is popular because it has structure and order, where much of the substantive post itself can be messy and unstructured. Automating sentiment measures is challenging, particularly on tweets where slang, symbols, images and excessive use of emoticons and punctuation is troublesome. No wonder, then, researchers stick to the metadata over the substance of the post itself.

While it appears that the majority of research focuses on the metadata over the data of social media, there are increased opportunities to work with the text of the posts themselves. Long-established Computer-Aided Qualitative Data Analysis Software (CAQDAS) packages like NVIVO have integrated the ability to ingest and to some extent code social media. With this a new generation of text analytic tools are being created specifically to work with social media text. One of the longer established is DiscoverText (Beyer, 2012; DiscoverText, 2013; Lu & Shulman, 2008;

Shulman, 2011, 2012; Shulman, 2009). This tool was first developed by researchers at the University of Massachusetts to help the US government process 'form letters', where public agencies receive several hundreds of thousands of almost identical letters as part of organised campaigns. The software would speed up the time it takes officials to process the letters by clustering near-identical letters and highlighting unique aspects.

The work culminated in a tool called DiscoverText, designed to allow several coders to work on a single dataset with checks to ensure inter-coder reliability and validity. Although DiscoverText now contains many features, its main point of departure from other CAQDAS packages is that it encourages coding to be performed in a series of passes, with a deliberately simple codebook. Coders are shown an item – a tweet, post or message – and might be asked to code simply whether the item is about the topic of interest – Yes/No. Coders are able to work through several thousand tweets in this way. Where large datasets are involved, researchers might choose to train up a Bayesian machine classifier to learn from the coding patterns.

Researchers from the Health Media Collabatory at UIC Chicago's Institute of Health Research and Policy have pioneered this approach (Kim, 2013). In one project they explore how anti-smoking campaigns are discussed online. Their approach is to capture smoking-related posts from a range of platforms. This kind of work presents a range of challenges in terms of both capturing and managing high volume archives, and then analysing them as datasets. Understanding what is being said about smoking on social media depends on both the ability to draw in a diversity of platforms and to understand how smoking is labelled. This requires an ever-evolving set of keywords: *cigs, cigarettes, fags, squares.* More than capturing a single hashtag, it requires a sensitivity to changing slang and colloquialisms. In addition, the object of discussion might not be in the tweet but in the link or the discussion of a person who has commented previously on the topic. The challenge facing this type of research is how to mitigate against missing out on an important slice of the conversation. A good example of this is the rapid rise of electronic cigarettes (e-cigarettes). From around 2010 onwards, marketers sought to cash in on the growing interest in this new way of smoking, with new names and hashtags emerging daily. To only search for 'ecigs' would risk missing out on the conversation as terminology organically evolved. However, in a situation where labels are fluid and emergent it is impossible to capture everything. Limitations should be acknowledged and claims carefully expressed.

The other challenge facing projects like those described above is that not only can an activity have several labels, but a single label can have several meanings. Smoking can be used in reference to tobacco, men and women, BBQs and cannabis (Kim, 2013). There are ways in which these can be disambiguated through a combination of coding and machine classification, but it introduces an extra challenge to this kind of research. The cautious approach is to cast the net wide in order to capture everything and then refine it later, rather than narrow the keywords and risk missing out on a key aspect of the conversation. The section will now revisit the MyPCC case and apply capture and sift approaches.

Example part 2: Capturing #MyPCC

To capture the discussion of the PCC election on social media first required an understanding of what terms or labels people used. Unlike the smoking example, there were not many alternatives to the two main hashtags: #PCC and #MyPCC. Although some did use #PCCelection in the early phases, longer hashtags were rarely used. The length of the term Police and Crime Commissioner elections meant few used this on Twitter – PCC was shorter and relatively unique as a label.

To capture the data, a 'fetch' was set up from Twitter's API to collect tweets mentioning PCC and MyPCC. Tweets were collected every 15 minutes between 23rd October and 20th November. In total, 95,000 tweets were captured. In addition a further 1,200 items from Facebook pages were collected (see Appendix). The fetch for PCC and MyPCC brought in both hashtags and mentions of the terms within tweets; if the tweet contained both terms it would be harvested just once. By using the API it cannot be guaranteed that 100% of PCC tweets were collected. However, it is possible to cross-reference with 'full firehose' indexes during this period. Based on cross-references with historic power track feeds on Topsy.com, in this case around 85% of tweets were captured.

Although MyPCC was globally unique, PCC was also used in other countries during the fetch. PCC was a name of a user in Indonesia, and was used as a tag to promote a music video for a band from Brazil. Furthermore, shortly after the election the Leveson enquiry into press standards generated discussion on the Press Complaints Commission. Therefore the challenge became how to filter out alternative meanings of the term PCC, in order to focus solely on the conversation surrounding the Police and Crime Commissioner elections. The tipping point in the data collected was 19th November, three days after the election result, when over half were overseas references to PCC and a large proportion of the remainder related to the Press Complaints Commission.

When tweets are collected in this way using the API, both the tweet and additional metadata is collected. In its rawest form the tweet and related metadata can be downloaded as a comma-separated file and opened as a spreadsheet. Each tweet has a row and additional columns include the date and time created, the name of the author, hashtags used, any other users mentioned, any URLs mentioned and, if compressed, the compressed URL. It also lists geo-coordinates; although in the case of the PCC archive, fewer than 1% had location services activated on their phone, some were recorded.

Using the captured data on PCC it was first possible to focus on the activity and interaction of policy actors. Of particular interest for this study was the role of the official feed of the Home Office as the lead agency for the PCC election. Tweeting as @UKHomeOffice, by the time of the election they had tweeted 1,500 times. They followed just a few other users, mainly other government departments, and had amassed 48,000 followers. Much of this information is publicly available, as Twitter is a public website; however, the Home Office, like any user, can delete their tweets, and any tweets directed at the user will not be explicitly shown in the Home Office timeline unless they quote or retweet it. On the other hand, capturing the full transaction enables us to examine the practices of a government department as it initiates a policy idea.

The PCC archive shows that the main focus of @UKHomeOffice was to publicise the election during the days leading up to polling day. Their activity linked to TV advertisements, YouTube videos, websites and their associated pictures on a dedicated photo sharing page provided by Flickr.com. Some attempts were also made to link with TV shows carrying the advertisements. In the early days of the MyPCC campaign, the tweets featured photographs of people holding up handwritten boards saying what they would like 'their PCC to do'.

Having a searchable archive makes it possible to focus on days when this campaign was active, and to investigate how others were engaging with it. The archive also shows that the Home Office made relatively little use of retweeting, possibly because to do so might be interpreted as endorsement, and perhaps because such retweeting usually requires authorisation. Where retweets were made, it tended to be messages from the prime minister or BBC news.

It is also possible to focus on retweets either for a particular user or in terms of overall numbers. With regard to a particular user, it might be useful to see if their campaign gained traction and spread virally through Twitter. It is also possible to see who was retweeting the message. Retweets are often (but not always) endorsements. The Home Office depended on other users retweeting their messages in order to most effectively reach a wider audience. A user with many followers and with a track record of these users retweeting their messages is important to a social media campaign such as MyPCC. In the case of MyPCC, it is possible to identify 256 unique users retweeting at least one Home Office tweet, and a group of 17 who loyally retweeted three or more. As discussed in the previous section, counting retweets is only one part of the picture, as much depends on whether these users have any engaged followers themselves. This is where exposure and page impression metrics can be considered. Another reason to focus on retweets might be to ascertain whether a particular tweet has been retweeted disproportionately. The exemplar here is the photo of Obama upon winning the 2012 US election with the caption 'Four more years', which became the most retweeted tweet in the history of Twitter, with over 810,000 retweets (Obama, 2012).

Using DiscoverText, the process of identifying the proportion of retweets involves de-duplicating the archive. When a tweet is retweeted it is textually identical and is only distinguished by its metadata, which will vary by time and user. Focusing on the first 54,000 tweets of those captured during the build-up the to election, the duplication report identified a tiny elite of tweets that had been retweeted more than 100 times each, giving these messages a broader exposure. Table 6.2 shows the five most retweeted messages, showing that four of the five had been sent by influential users including the Home Office, the prime minister, John Prescott (former deputy prime minister under New Labour government and PCC candidate), and the BBC.

The user '@Laptop_cop' is perhaps the standout here. This is the tweet of a frontline police officer who blogs under the pseudonym of Laptop Cop and had around 2,500 followers at the time of the retweet. The top five served different purposes. The Prescott tweet did not defame the policy as such, but did take an opportunity to suggest that the organisation was poor. @laptop_cop was arguing for independent candidates over party politics. The prime minister and Home Office endorsed the policy and both BBC and Home Office helped to share more information about the election. It is also worth noting that 46,000 of 54,000 tweets issued during the build-up to the election were single items: they were not retweeted by anybody. If the average Twitter user is estimated to have 208 followers (Smith, 2013) then the maximum number of page

Table 6.2 The five most retweeted tweets of the PCC election

		RTs (RTs captured by API)
1	John Prescott (Labour candidate) 'Unbelievable! Coalition incompetence means #PCC ballots costing £350,000 will have to be shredded'	71 (71) Anti-organiser
2	@BBCEngland (Media organisation): The #PCC elections take place in two days, find out about the candidates in your area on the BBC's special page	60 (56) Info
3	@laptop_cop (Police blogger): I think that voting for a #PCC that's backed by a political party will only do more harm than good #NoPlaceForPo	60 (55) Anti-party/Pro-inde
4	@David_Cameron (Prime Minster): Inspiring visit to @LivingWellTrust in Carlisle with the local #PCC candidate @RhodesRr	53 (43) Pro-PCC
5	@ukhomeoffice (Home Office): #MyPCC will focus on the things I care about. What will yours do? Vote on 15 Nov. Please RT	55 (42) Info/Pro-PCC

impressions of these non-retweeted tweets will be limited to an average of 208. Furthermore, only 430 tweets of the set of 54,000 were retweeted more than five times. Some of these might be alternative versions of the themes raised in these top tweets, but this would require further work (discussed below).

But much of this can be found using 'monitor and visualise' techniques. With subscription to such tools it is possible to search through several months of tweets using historic power track or indexed data. It is also possible to identify these top tweets in terms of the number of times they were retweeted or discussed. But having these data in an archive permits further exploration and enquiry. It is an historic record.

Retweets are only part of the picture. Users of Twitter will often quote a tweet and prefix or suffix the message with one of their own. They sometimes also modify the original tweet. Some follow a convention of using the label MT for modified tweet, but not all do so. The ease by which users of Twitter can modify or append tweets is akin to the problem of the public agency that is required to sift through 10,000 near-identical form letters. The way around this is to identify not only duplicates, but also near-duplicates.

The identification of near-duplicates, using DiscoverText's clustering algorithm, works by setting a threshold for what constitutes a duplicate. De-duplicating tweets is a process of clustering. The choice of threshold depends on the motivation in the research design. A common motivation would be reductionist – to strip out near-identical tweets to speed up coding. Alternatively the research design might seek to preserve greater heterogeneity of the near-identical tweets to better understand nuances. In practice, the clusters bring together almost identical tweets, where usually just one or two words have been added as prefixes or suffixes to a message from another user, and thereby changing the meaning. Clustering begins by first accounting for the exact duplicates (retweets).

In the PCC case of the first 54,000 tweets, 6,000 were found to be duplicates. A further 6,229 clusters of near-identical tweets were then identified as near-duplicates. Heading each of these clusters is a 'seed' item, usually the tweet that has been subject to modification by the creators of the other tweets in the cluster. An example from the PCC case, of where the clustering picked up modification, enhancement or subversion of messages, is a tweet sent by the prime minister, who tweeted on the morning of the election, 15 November 2012: 'We're helping police forces be more accountable. I've voted in the first ever PCC elections. I hope you do too.' In addition to some users retweeting this in unmodified form, other users retweeted this to their followers with a variety of additional prefixes, 'Most won't…' or suffixes such as '…or I will look silly', 'whatever!', 'Labour', 'jog on', with others creating semantic hashtags such as '#seriousdislike'.

The identification of cluster seeds and related clusters of near-identical items reveals much about how users interact with policy issues on Twitter, as well as some of the challenges of analysing the data. It reveals the use of spam. It reveals how, when mainstream news agencies offer 'share' buttons on their stories, URL link shorteners vary and therefore create near-identical tweets. It reveals how campaign groups send the same message several times to various key policy actors, or bloggers direct messages at high profile users, asking them to 'read and RT'. It also reveals the circulation of petitions and images designed to undermine the policy.

Clustering aids a reductionist strategy by reducing the number of tweets required for coding or classification, but it is important to investigate how tweets in each of the largest clusters are being modified in order to capture important patterns of subversion or support. The main motivation for clustering might be just that: to understand and compare the clustering of an issue. The PCC example showed that the vast majority of tweets were single items that were not retweeted. But not all policy issues would be clustered in this way. A suggested comparator measure could be to use the H-index, as used in measuring academic citations: 'h-index is the largest number h such that h publications have at least h citations' (Harzing & van der Wal, 2009). For example, in the PCC case, 24 clusters of duplicates had 24 or more items (an H-index score of 24). In the near-duplicates, 20 contained more than 20 items. By focusing on the H-index it is possible to compare across policy ideas to determine the degree to which the issue is beginning to crystallise around a limited number of viewpoints. It also reveals whether any particular tweet is dominating in the dataset. While the PCC case showed this not to be the case, other policy ideas have higher H-index scores (see Appendix, Table 9.4).

Metadata

Many examples of social movements, including use of Twitter in the Arab spring, or processes of cascading messages following natural disasters, demonstrate the power of individual tweets to mobilise action. Other examples, such as the subversion of the prime minister's tweet (described above), or where users add cartoons or humorous photos, display mischief and humour rather than potentially mobilising masses. In the case of the PCC election, however, it appears from de-duplication that there was no organic groundswell around any particular theme. Instead, clusters in the PCC case are mainly self-promotional – buy my book, read my blog, or respond to the specific interest of my organisation. In the case of the PCC elections, at least, it appears through this form of analysis that there was no moment where a celebrity or high profile user helped to cascade that 'killer tweet'. That is not to say that people did not try; for example, one user tweeted at Stephen Fry, a British writer and TV personality with, at that time, over six million followers: '@stephenfry Hope now US elections are over momentum carries to UK #MyPCC elections! Can u help? I'm working on: [Link to content]'.

As discussed above, with every item of social media data comes additional metadata. Depending on the type of analysis, this metadata is of varying interest. The public API includes the user's Followers and Friends count, the date and time of each tweet, hashtags used, source (phone type/web), URL mentioned and expanded, bio, location, website and real name. It also includes number of tweets 'favourited'. If this is not enough, researchers can use full firehose feeds to also acquire Klout scores, rule match (the fetch rule that brought it in), number of tweets made, and the real name of any people mentioned.

In DiscoverText researchers might want to focus on filtering by metadata, for example, creating a dataset focused only on users with a 'Klout' score of 65 or more. In previous work filtering in this way represented only 1% of the tweets of the dataset (see Appendix). Users of this order have more than 3,000 followers, but the score is also calculated on the proportion of their several thousand tweets that are retweeted. Where users have linked to other accounts it also considers their use of other platforms such as Facebook. The appeal of filtering by Klout is that only 'influential' people and their tweets are included. It can cut out those 85% of tweets that are retweeted by nobody. Through this filter, it is possible to identify the influential views of opinion shapers.

DiscoverText includes a TopMeta explorer that is used to get an overview of a particular dataset or archive. Here it is possible to determine that #PCC was the most used hashtag (39,647) while #PCCelections was only used 1,504 times; who the top ten tweets came from; that the most tweets from a single user was 350; the most shared URLs in their expanded form; and the users who were most often mentioned (Prime Minister David Cameron and two of the candidates using Twitter in their election campaign, Ann Barnes and John Prescott). The main benefit of the TopMeta values is to get a quick overview and understanding of what is happening in the data – what, if anything, is dominating. It could also flag up spam or unrelated tweets. The TopMeta function can also be used to advise the researcher what hashtags to focus on, what people to follow or what keywords to add to fetches.

From the TopMeta explorer, the most popular tweets and the most often-shared link will show certain themes that are emerging, and these are further revealed by focusing on the most used terms, displayed as a word cloud. The word clouds flag up unusual words or terms that might say something of how the policy is developing. For example, one word relatively unusual in normal language but commonly used in the PCC case was 'farce'. It was used in different ways: low turnout, poor design, politicisation, organisation and information were all themes used in conjunction with the idea of the election of PCCs as farce. For example:

- Just voted, polling station staff told me I was number 38 out of the 600-odd registered #pcc #farce

- RT @[user]: If independent #pcc has no cash how would they improve on the current election farce? Sponsorship perhaps...oops there goes independence
- @user Its a farce that your party wanted to bring politics into policing. Feels like your creating a 65k retirement home #pcc [sic]
- Loving this brand new epetition re the #pcc farce. [link]
- The PCC election is a farce. No info provided by gov or candidates and they want my vote? #PCC

Given the continually changing context of the discussion across social media, it is perhaps most useful to use word clouds at points throughout the period of collection rather than at the end of the process. The archive can be filtered, for example, fortnightly, weekly or daily, to show the 50, 100 or 150 most used words in a given period. Certain usernames, personalities and hashtags will dominate but certain themes will also become clear. This approach can reveal subtle changes in emphasis as well as the arrival and, importantly, the departure of certain words and terms associated with the policy idea.

Figure 6.7 draws on the first two weeks of activity and the first 18,000 tweets collected related to the PCC election. PCC appears in four-fifths of the dataset and MyPCC appears in a quarter of the dataset. Words that could sustain the campaign include *campaigning, choose, community, engage, forward, hope, huge, listen, look, meeting, value* and *vote*. There are words that could undermine the campaign, such as *can't* (often used in reference to 'can't find anything about the candidate in my area')

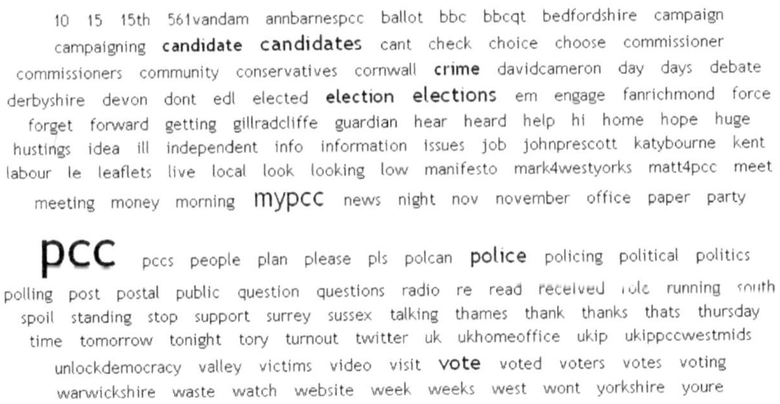

10 15 15th 561vandam annbarnespcc ballot bbc bbcqt bedfordshire campaign campaigning **candidate candidates** cant check choice choose commissioner commissioners community conservatives cornwall **crime** davidcameron day days debate derbyshire devon dont edl elected **election elections** em engage fanrichmond force forget forward getting gillradcliffe guardian hear heard help hi home hope huge hustings idea ill independent info information issues job johnprescott katybourne kent labour le leaflets live local look looking low manifesto mark4westyorks matt4pcc meet meeting money morning mypcc news night nov november office paper party pcc pccs people plan please pls polcan police policing political politics polling post postal public question questions radio re read received role running south spoil standing stop support surrey sussex talking thames thank thanks thats thursday time tomorrow tonight tory turnout twitter uk ukhomeoffice ukip ukippccwestmids unlockdemocracy valley victims video visit vote voted voters votes voting warwickshire waste watch website week weeks west wont yorkshire youre

Figure 6.7   Honeymoon cloud: first fortnight of the PCC campaign
Source: DiscoverText.com.

and with some attempts at stopping the election through the establish-
ment of a 'stop pcc election' petition, Facebook groups and a #stoppcc
hashtag. However, these failed to gather much momentum in terms of
signatures or followers. *Turnout* also features. Overall, this is a cloud
focused on education and information – 'check out my website', 'check
the list of candidates in your area'. This unidirectional broadcasting
from both the Home Office and the candidates is similar to the communication style of the airline companies and charities discussed in the
previous chapter.

In the second cloud, Figure 6.8 based on the week before the election, the frequency of tweets has doubled. This cloud is based on
15,600 tweets where now an eighth rather than a quarter of the dataset
includes MyPCC. Potentially supportive terms remain: *agree, choice,
debate, democracy, hope, local, luck, unlockdemocracy*. But *low* and *turnout*
also feature and a new term – *spoil* – makes an appearance in the top
150. Also new to the cloud are mentions of smaller political parties –
EDL (English Defence League) and UKIP – and the term *waste*, all of
which feature in the moral debate about the implications of not voting
or spoiling the ballot. Despite this shift in emphasis, the focus remains
on prominent candidates, information giving and publicity.

15 15th actually agree annbarnespcc ballot bbc bbcqt bedfordshire campaign
campaigning **candidate candidates** cant check chief choice commissioner
commissioners community congresso conservatives cornwall **crime** cuts
davidcameron day days debate democracy derbyshire devon **dont** edl
elected **election elections** em experience force forget free getting
government guardian guide hear heard help hi home hope hustings idea
ill independent info information job johnprescott kent labour leaflet leaflets
lib lit live local look looking low luck manifesto mark4westyorks message
money morning **mypcc** news night norfolk nov november office officers
online page paper parties party **pcc** pccelections pccs people
person please pls **police** policing political politics polling post postal
privatisation public questions radio re read remember role running send
share special spoil standing support sussex talk thanks thats thurs thursday
time **tomorrow** tomorrows tonight tony tory turnout ukhomeoffice ukip
unlockdemocracy visit **vote** voted voters votes voting warwickshire waste
website week west win wont yorkshire youre

Figure 6.8   Storm cloud: the week before the PCC election
Source: DiscoverText.com.

10 10pm 1st 20 actually agree ballot believe bit bothered candidate candidates cant cast chance check choice close commissioner count crime cry davidcameron day democracy democratic didnt doesnt dont elected **election** **elections** farce feel fn forget funny getting haha hard havent heard help home hope hour hours id idea ill independent individual info information job kent labour laugh laughed left liked little local lol look looking looks love low luck maybe money morning mypcc news none

norfolk omfg omg paper particular party **pcc** pccelections pccs people person please **police** policing political politics poll **polling** polls poor post privatisation public quiet read real remember results role seen specific spoil spoiled spoiling spoilt staff standing station stations support sussex tell thanks thats theres time todays tomorrow tonight tories tory turnout twitter uk ukip **um** video **video** **vote** **voted** votelabour voter voters votes voting wales waste west win **wins** wonder wont wtf youre

Figure 6.9 Polling cloud: the day of the election
Source: DiscoverText.com.

The third cloud, Figure 6.9 captures activity on the day of the election when schools were closed to serve as polling stations. The cloud is based on the hours of polling – 6am to 10pm, drawing on a dataset of 23,000 tweets. MyPCC features in less than a 10th of the dataset. Words reflect the activity of voting: *cast, choice, local, democracy, democratic, please, voted*. The term *spoil*, found in the previous cloud, is joined by its variants *spoiled, spoiling* and *spoilt*. In terms of words that could undermine the election, *farce* appears for the first time, as did *bothered, omg/omfg* (oh my god) and *wtf* (what the f**k). The term *privatisation* also features; a further reason to spurn the PCC election was the suggestion that PCCs would enable the Coalition Government to legitimise the privatisation of further aspects of the police force.

The word clouds offer a means to identify important tweets. Rather than identifying the single viral tweet that changed the direction of the discussion, the aim is to identify the beginnings of meme-like story-lines that circulate in various forms and variants.

Conclusion

This chapter has explored the challenge of capturing social media discussion of policy ideas. The chapter explored how platforms are permitting third party applications for text analytics to index, synthesise and visualise streams of social media data. The chapter divided this terrain into two areas of activity. The first was 'monitor and visualise'.

These activities permit real-time surveillance. The example of the interview with the BBC's George Entwistle was offered to highlight the real implications of a senior official not being aware of how their organisation is discussed online. We can see how this ability to visualise is of interest to those predicting uprisings or speculating on the outcomes of elections, and to those trying to understand what is important to report, how human behaviour is changing or whose brands are sinking and whose are on the rise.

What these spheres share is a need for real-time insight, and these tools are attractive to users seeking a quick visualisation of what is occurring. The chapter described a booming and immature industry, suggesting further acquisitions, consolidations, mergers and name changes in the coming years as the social media customer insight business develops.

The chapter explored how public services might avail of such services for managing their social media interaction. We also saw how this could have been useful to the Home Office when implementing the PCC election. They would have been able to see what was important, which influential actors were getting involved, and what exposure the issue was having. They would have seen that their official hashtag was having limited exposure. These tools would have also indicated the net balance of positive against negative tweets around their official hashtag. But we also saw the limitation of this approach in terms of how long a tweet remains current, as well as the limitations and dangers of blindly trusting the sentiment meters.

The alternative to 'monitor and visualise' is to 'capture and sift'. The latter approach involves recording and capturing, scraping and harvesting, drawing the data onto computer servers for the purpose of analysis. This section explored how in a single day several thousand items could be collected, each with additional metadata. The 'capture and sift' approach offered insights into how particular users were tweeting, and enabled a focus on the most retweeted tweets. It explored the kinds of clusters of near-duplicates that were present, and whether particular clustered tweets were dominating an archive. In short, it can reveal the practices and tactics used by users to publicise projects or products.

The chapter explored how metadata around influence metrics (such as a Klout score) can reveal the practices of influential users; how TopMeta functions can reveal key people and popular linked content. A focus on word frequencies and word clouds can be used to offer periodic snapshots of emerging themes and sentiment. This is not a one click sentiment meter, but rather the starting point for designing codesets or machine classification criteria. It is to this end we turn in the next chapter.

The case explored in this chapter was the PCC election. What both the 'monitor and visualise' and 'capture and sift' approaches revealed is harsh criticism of the organisers of the election that was borne out in later evaluations (Electoral Commission, 2013) and perhaps reflected in the final turnout in the election. But the extent to which social media helped to fuel this is difficult to measure. The next chapter will explore how a deeper analysis can be conducted.

7
Interpreting Social Media Data

This chapter is all about the challenge of interpreting and ascribing the meaning of social media data. The challenge is brought into sharp relief by court judgements where teams of lawyers spent weeks poring over the meaning of tweets in order to determine if they were threatening or libellous (see Paul Chambers, 'or I'm blowing the Airport Skyhigh' tweet in January 2010 or Sally Bercow's '*Innocent face*' tweet that led to a trial in May 2013). The question of this chapter is: what is happening on the days when a policy idea is widely discussed? The frequency charts profiled in Chapter 6 show dramatic fluctuations in activity directed to specific policy ideas. This raises questions as to what is occurring within that variation. It also raises questions as to what themes are contained within that activity; which of it is new that day; which of it is a continuation of themes from previous days. This chapter focuses on exploring this activity so that we can begin to understand the lifecycle of policy ideas when they are discussed online.

In response to the challenges of interpreting social media data, the chapter explores how a combination of human and machine classification can be deployed to a dataset of social media data discussing a policy idea. It has three sections. The first explores the challenge of coding and specifically separating out opinion from other kinds of posts (such as information or questions). The second section then explores how opinionated tweets can be classified into themes. The third section explores a range of ways in which this classified data can then be used to answer a range of research questions. How are themes changing and sustaining over time? How do themes vary across source? And what shared viewpoints are crystallising within this diversity of debate? Overall, the chapter argues that such data are challenging for policy analysis, but also highly revealing.

Crowdsourced coding

In qualitative research, researchers use a codebook of codes to mark passages of datasets and thereby allocate a category or theme. This is coding. Programmes like NVIVO or Atlas TI are labelled as part of the CAQDAS family of applications. While more commonly used for coding interview transcripts or fieldnotes, the capability of coding photographs and social media items improves with each new version of the software. This section explores how software can be used to code and classify the data for the purposes of understanding and analysing evolving policy ideas.

The previous chapter discussed how one CAQDAS programme, DiscoverText, could be used to capture social media data. DiscoverText has been designed to allow researchers to break the coding task up into manageable pieces. Its developers critique the conventional CAQDAS programmes that find coders using elaborate multi-tiered codesets (defined sets of codes), with 30 or 40 different codes and categories. Instead it considers the human capacity to hold up to seven things in the head at one time. It encourages coding exercises involving a series of 'passes' of the dataset.

In a series of passes, pass one could be, 'Is this tweet about the policy'? with two codes, Yes or No. One hundred tweets could be coded in ten minutes. The task can then be allocated to a team. The degree of coder agreement could be assessed and overall validity of the codes adjudicated. A second pass could focus on sentiment – is this pro-, anti- or neutral towards the policy? A third pass could introduce a set of themes. Each of these passes uses a codeset. The patterns from the human coding can be used as training data to inform a Bayesian machine classifier. The classifier works on the basis of confidence intervals and can be used to suggest with variable certainty how uncoded items should be coded, thereby speeding up the coding tasks.

While coding social media posts using single-digit codesets might be designed to be simple, it is not without challenges. The task requires shared understanding of what constitutes a topic-related post and how to identify story-lines. The approach brings up issues of definition. On what do you base your definition; in what ways can and should it be revised? What are the practicalities of a single coder coding 1,000, 2,000 or 50,000 items? If engaging multiple coders, how can you be certain the coders have a shared definition of what is a story-line and what is not? How can inter-coder agreement (reliability) and overall accuracy (validity) be adjudicated? In what ways and to what limits can machine-based coding or machine classifiers be utilised?

This section responds to these questions of definition, as well as the practicalities and implications of engaging multiple coders and the possibilities of machine classification. Following from the previous chapter, it draws further on the archive of the first 54,000 tweets collected during the run up to the PCC election in November 2012, introduced in the previous chapter. The research process is described, and the analysis initially focuses on the PCC case, before extending it to include consideration of two further policy ideas: Compassionate Care and the Bedroom Tax.

To code the PCC archive, a team of four coders was recruited (a further three coders joined the team later). Each was given a DiscoverText account and provided with an information sheet outlining the purpose of the project. Then they were all allocated a dataset called PCC50, a randomly generated set of 50 tweets from the PCC election. The coders were issued with a simple coding scheme – 1. Statement, 2. Not Statement. The information sheet outlined a brief definition of what constituted a statement of opinion and not a statement of opinion, in terms of suitability for inclusion in a Q methodology study (Chapter 4). At this point in the project the definitions were very simple. An example of guidance given to coders of the PCC50 dataset was:

- Tweets that should be coded as statements of opinion may include some of the following:

  o Tweets: suggesting the PCC election or PCCs is/are a waste of money; politicisation of the police; election less popular than a TV show; low priority in media; lack of information or funding of a mailshot; legitimation of spoiling ballot; campaign to spoil ballot or shame government about this; reminders that only voters have the right to complain or that voting is a hard won privilege or duty.

  o Terms to look for: 'I reckon'; 'I wonder'; 'can we'; 'is it just me...'; or they quote others with a message they agree with,

- Examples of what we think are NOT statements:

  o The other two-thirds of tweets are better described as broadcasting information or conversational.

  o They might include promotion or celebration of particular candidates, statistical predictions about results, description of campaigning activities, questions as part of conversation, discussion that seems completely unrelated to the election, reports of links to websites, open questions to followers, direct questions to candidates, short responses as part of conversations, facts or responses to direct questions, rumours, acknowledgement and thanks, reminders, appeals.

Coders were directed to news coverage of the policy idea to aid familiarity. At this point coders were not instructed to look for specific 'story-lines' as described by (Hajer, 1995, 2010), but rather given examples of what might constitute a statement of opinion about PCC and what might not. At this point in the process the primary intention was to introduce the coders to the specific conventions of Twitter discussed above.

The five coders took between 15 and 40 minutes to code the first dataset of 50 items. The project manager also coded data sets alongside the main role of creating and allocating datasets. The next step was to adjudicate the coding. Each item was reviewed in turn. In the case of most items, the coding decision was unanimous, and the code could be validated accordingly. In a few cases the decision was split. When validating the coding of five coders there are two types of disagreement. The 4v1 split is where a single coder differs from the others. In this situation it is necessary to offer direct feedback with each coder, giving them an opportunity to reflect on the decision. The second type of split with five coders is 3v2, or a 60–40 split. It is the role of the researcher to adjudicate whether to follow a majority verdict or to go with the minority. In most situations the decision is relatively straightforward. All of the 3v2 tweets and the validation decisions were fed back collectively to the coders, offering them the opportunity to discuss the decision.

By adjudicating the coding decisions it was possible to determine the percentage of agreement between coders. With the first dataset (PCC50) the overall level of agreement was 88% based on five coders. However, it was also clear that within this figure, the agreement around what was a Statement was less than 80%. The aim of this preliminary part of the process was to incorporate feedback on split decisions and improve definitions in the guidance for coders, with the aim of improving the level of agreement in the second round of coding.

Following the adjudication of the first dataset of 50 items, an updated codebook was prepared and circulated to all coders. The codebook included a clearer definition of the two codes, this time expressing what was sought in terms of story-lines. The codebook included examples of adjudicated tweets from the first dataset to help reinforce the distinction.

The new codebook included the following definitions:

- Topic (of the study): The principal matter or singular focus of the study. (In this current research the topic is the decision to hold elections to decide who should become the first elected PCCs in 41 local police areas.)
- On-topic/Off-topic tweet: Discusses topic of study or does not discuss topic of study.
- Story-line: A story-line is a short two or three word opinionated phrase. Story-lines are ritualised and often clichéd tropes, figures of speech or slogans that serve to aid the reduction of complexity and give a certain permanence to the debate (Hajer, 1995, p. 63). Examples of story-lines in the current study could include: 'prioritising gone to pot', 'so little publicity', 'zero information'.
- Q Statement: 'A definite or clear expression of opinion, usually around 15 words, used as stimuli in Q methodology. When drawn from tweets statements are either direct quotes (naturalistic) or formed from a story-line and the semantic context within which it was uttered (modified)'.
- Q sort: A procedure where participants are given 30 or 40 statements written out on cards and asked to rank them in order of most like and most unlike their point of view (see www.qmethod.org).
- A tweet to be coded as a statement: On-topic opinion or including contextualised story-lines.
- A tweet to be coded as non-statement: One that is completely off-topic or contains story-lines directed towards off-topic, or on-topic but reporting only factual information or general conversation.

What emerged from this collective approach to coding was how a statement of opinion could be adapted from a tweet. In the initial information sheet, coders were instructed to distinguish between tweets that conveyed opinion and those that expressed information or engaged in conversation. What the early coding revealed was how tweets could contain all of these elements, and how an opinionated story-line could be expressed in a single hashtag. Through the introduction of the codebook, coders were next briefed to code by identifying story-lines within tweets.

This leads us to the question of what the tweet contained that particularly resonated? A tweet will often engage satire, humour, parody or irony. It captures the thinking of a wider group. I would argue that what is likely to be present in this tweet is a story-line. Maarten Hajer defines these as crisp generative statements (1995, p. 68). They might not be new, they are often rather cliché, but they resonate and help to convey a message. In the medium of a tweet, where character length is restricted, story-lines offer a shorthand to convey sentiment; tweets can contain both policy ideas and story-lines about them. An example of expressing an opinion with a story-line might be: 'I think the introduction of elected #PCCs is politicising our police force. I won't be voting'. As discussed in the previous chapter, numerous variants of this tweet might be sent over the course of the discussion, but it is the defined name of the policy initiative and related activities condensed to #PCC, combined with the condensed argumentation of the story-line 'politicising the police' that is key to interpreting the meaning of a tweet.

Once coders had received and read the new codebook they were allocated a second dataset, consisting of 250 randomly allocated tweets (PCC250A). Coders spent between 40 and 90 minutes coding this second dataset. The coding was adjudicated as before, allowing for the identification and dissemination of 3v2 disputes, and one-to-one feedback on 4v1 splits. It was also possible to identify inter-coder agreement, which improved from 88.06% to 89.66%, the Fleiss kappa being 0.76 and 0.79 respectively (as shown in Tables 7.1 and 7.2). Coders whose agreement was below average were asked to reflect on their 4v1 splits. The coders varied from one that emerged as the '1' in three 4v1 splits, compared with another coder that was the '1' on 15 occasions. With this process of feedback, the overall level of agreement rose, and the accuracy of lower performing coders improved greatly, with one coder rising from 80% agreement in the first dataset to 92% in the second.

After coding the second dataset, coders were issued with details of coding disputes, and the codebook was again updated with improved definitions and additional examples to help to exemplify distinctions. At this point two additional coders were recruited to join the team.

Table 7.1 Comparing coding of six coders in dataset one PCC50

Code/Coder	A	B	C	D	E	F	Exact Match	Partial Match	kappa
Not statement	30	34	37	39	38	33	25	16	0.81
Statement	20	16	13	11	12	17	5	14	0.65
Totals	50	50	50	50	50	50	30	30	0.76

Table 7.2   Standard comparisons between coders in dataset two PCC250A

Code	B	C	D	E	F	Exact Match	Partial Match	kappa
Not statement	199	205	181	174	186	148	61	0.83
Statement	51	45	69	76	64	27	49	0.64
Totals	250	250	250	250	250	175	110	0.79

The new coders were initiated through the first two datasets before being exposed to the third dataset. The project now included a project manager and six coders, who then set about coding a third dataset (PCC250B) of 250 tweets, again, randomly drawn from the PCC archive. The adjudication of the coding of PCC250B showed marginal improvements in agreement and validity, but most importantly, it showed the team were sufficiently familiar with the policy issue and the task of coding policy-related tweets.

Moving to code a larger proportion of the dataset, this time coders were allocated individual batches of between 1,000 and 2,500. At this step a third code was added to the codebook, 'don't know'. The aim of this intervention was to avoid any delay in the coding process. Although it would have been possible to code up the full 46,000 tweets, the aim instead was to code up around a third of the tweets, using the output as training data for the Bayesian machine classifier. It is worth also adding at this point that the majority of tweets coded did not express opinion about PCCs: the coders determined that less than a fifth (18%) of the tweets were statements of opinion.

The coding of the remaining two-thirds of the PCC archive could then be performed by the machine classifier, with the classifier suggesting the most likely codes based on certainty thresholds. Although it is possible to apply the classifier using the training data, it is more accurate to begin with a subset of tweets with the highest degree of certainty of belonging to a particular code. The task is therefore to start the process by filtering by classification boundary in order to identify those at the 90% and 95% confidence levels and coding these first in sets of 100. This is known as coding by list, rather than the individual method used by coders. The approach of coding in sets of 100 is designed to allow the dataset to continue to be annotated, whilst at the same time training, customising and ultimately improving the accuracy of the machine classifier.

The capacity of a classifier – its potential to offer researchers valid classification tasks – will vary depending on the nature of the codeset. Success is reported by researchers at UIC Chicago in identifying different types of smoking discussion (Szczypka et al 2012; Kim, 2013). A similar technique could be used for sentiment or opinion. But unlike most automated classifiers, the validity of the classifiers can be verified. Designing a classifier that can distinguish opinion about one topic (view of PCC elections) from opinion about another (view of candidates) is perhaps a greater challenge. That said, where the agreement between coders is high, there is no reason why this learning cannot be used to train the classifier.

Thematic coding

The next section reports the process of how the opinionated tweets, distinguished in the first round of coding, were categorised by theme. The process started by initially free-coding the story-lines of each tweet. This process of allocating items to a code is widely applied in qualitative research (Bowen, 2008). In general, each new item is given a new code until the point of saturation at which no new codes are required. The next step is to consolidate codes to come up with a short list of themes that can be applied to the wider dataset. In order to accommodate the possibility of additional codes, a general category of 'other' can be introduced. Where the coder was unsure, a 'don't know' can be used in the early stages to prompt discussion. Because of the potential for some of the previous coding to be invalid, it is to be expected that some items may be rejected.

In the PCC case, a random set of 250 was generated from a set of 2,125 tweets validated as statements of opinion in the process described above. The initial free-coding generated 22 codes, which focused around five common themes: *lack of information, politicisation, quality of organisation, calibre of the candidates, questioning the right to vote*. Additional themes, such as a specific discussion of apathy to voters or questioning the turnout, also featured. A basic codebook defining the five codes was produced. It also included three further codes of *other, not statement* (of opinion) and *not sure*. The initial codebook definitions of the emergent themes of the PCC statement tweets were:

1. Information – likely to mention: 'no idea who', more info from pizza company, sarcastic use of hashtag like #blanketcoverage, 'so little

coverage', consideration for non-internet users, 'why should I have to find out', criticism of lack of response from candidates, reflection on how it was hard to find information on websites, not enough info to make decision.

2. Politicisation – Story-lines about keeping politics out of policing. Arguments against political parties dominating the election, disagreeing with using an election to appoint police officials. Slogans include no politics in policing, politicisation, they can't be independent if they are linked to parties, 'political appointments', politics has no place in PCCs, party politics 'stranglehold' on elections.

3. Organisation – this focuses on the Home Office or authorities in general as being to blame for a poor election. Likely to comment on quality of official websites, use phrases like shoddy or shambles, omishambles, dogs dinner, farce, train wreck, failure, 'can't blame candidates for Government not explaining it', 'Mugabe's election campaigns are better run', might suggest TV adverts are annoying or sensationalist.

4. Candidates – This predominately discusses the quality or suitability of the candidates – it might question or indeed celebrate the quality – it might say none of the candidates have right background, or right experience or knowledge, they don't understand issues/specifics, policing in hands of amateurs, need for more vetting, too few women/too many men, too many politicos, inadequate – limited vision/strategic depth.

5. Use Vote – These statements tend to argue that you have to use your vote, even if you don't fully agree with the election. They might say exercise your right to a vote, remember those that fought and died for the vote we now enjoy, #suffragettes, it might attempt to warn those who might not vote by saying you are 'turning your back on the frightened and vulnerable', or will let in extremist or smaller parties such as UKIP or the EDL, 'don't complain afterwards', 'not voting makes it worse', A PCC with less mandate is worst of all worlds, 'democracy is fragile elsewhere'. Or might also say – don't vote and it will be scrapped.

6. Other – there are likely to be minority discussions that do not easily fit into one of the above. Might include – not important, accountability, cost, illegitimate election, focus on victims, privatisation, distraction, red tape.

7. Not Statement – Use this code if you query that this is not a statement of opinion about the PCC election. Therefore it will be sent for

further coding. It is likely that between 20–30% of statements will fit into this category.
8. Not sure – if you don't know what it is trying to argue, code this.

Using the initial codebook, three coders coded the 250 items. The level of agreement varied considerably between codes. For some codes the agreement was high, particularly *information* and *politicisation*, but the opportunity for coders to select three codes: *not statement*, *don't know* and *other* meant coders had three codes by which to dispose of uncertainties. The poorer levels of agreement indicated there was too much flexibility in this set.

In preparing for the next round of coding the coders all gave written feedback on the experience. After further discussion an additional code was added, for statements about the cost of the elections. The definitions of each code were revised. One of the main issues was how some tweets included more than one theme. Although there is an option of coding the same items using two or more codes, it was decided to ask coders to focus on what they considered to be the principal theme of the tweet. An alternative would have been to introduce a new code called 'mixed.' The main purpose of this codeset piloting is to foster common agreement between the research team.

In order to test the revised thematic codeset, a random set of 100 items was sent to coders. The Kappa scores showed a modest improvement, however, given the variety of codes, it had to be accepted that perfect agreement was not possible, as it was in the simple binary of yes/no in the first round of coding.

The coders continued to code a broader set of 2,000 items. The coding revealed that just over a quarter were about lack of information about the elections (26%), just under a quarter about using the vote (23%), and the remaining tweets focused on politicisation (17%), organisers (15%), candidates (11%) and cost (8%).

Thematic exploration

This section now explores a variety of approaches whereby thematic coding can be used as a source of data for further insight and analysis into the shape of ideas. The three approaches discussed below include:

1. Informing a chronological insight into the changing shape of policy ideas;
2. Offering the basis for comparison of sources;

3. Contributing to a sample of statements to crowdsource shared viewpoints using online Q methodology.

Approach 1: Chronological insight

The thematic coding of PCC tweets can be illustrated by a stacked area graph (Figure 7.1), plotting the frequency of tweets during the build-up to the PCC election. The stacked area graph shows layers of themes, with a seam for each theme. The top line traces the daily fluctuation of activity around the PCC discussion during the course of the election. Importantly, this is not quite the same as 'activity' overall. This is the fluctuation of discussion of PCC as a policy rather than a fluctuation of discussion about PCC candidates standing in the the election.

Below the top line we find thematic seams. The five main themes developed in the initial codebook were mentioned at least once a day. The plot shows how, every day, somebody expressed an opinion towards

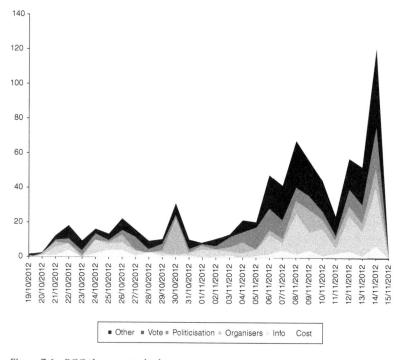

Figure 7.1   PCC themes stacked
Source: 1135 opinionated PCC tweets coded by theme (3 coders, validated).

the PCC policy idea using one of these five core themes. Some days certain themes were greater than others. For example, 30th October saw a set of tweets expressing discussion of the organisers. And on 8th November there was a focus on the quality of the information provided about the elections.

The seam representing the 'other' theme is worthy of particular attention. As the volume of tweets increased around the point of the election, this category grew disproportionately as mainstream media attention increased their coverage, and greater audiences were commenting on the policy. A third of the 'other' tweets were made on a single day over the three week period of the study – the day of the results (16th November). Table 7.3 gives a sense of the diversity of story-lines featuring in the 'other' tweets. Unlike the five core themes displayed in Figure 7.1 these were not applied with the same consistency, but collectively they add to an accumulation of meaning surrounding the PCC election, akin to the stylised depiction of the Flourishing Neighbourhoods policy idea featured in Chapter 3 (see Figure 3.4).

Approach 2: Comparison of sources

It is difficult to ascertain whether or not a data source offers comprehensive coverage of a debate surrounding a policy idea. Twitter data are often cast as being of limited use to social science, in that they are too narrow and do not reflect the wider conversation or public opinion. The argument goes that the demographic of people using Twitter mean that it is a liberal platform. Additionally, arguments circulate that many of its reported 400m accounts are dormant or fake, that many of its users are passive recipients of information who rarely tweet. There are also suggestions made against Twitter for its brevity, arguing against the potential for qualitative enquiry. These arguments, extended to the discussion of policy ideas, suggest that drawing only on Twitter would mean that the discussion of policy would be insufficiently comprehensive.

For instance, Mitchell & Hitlin (2013) argue that Twitter reaction to events is often at odds with overall public opinion. The claim of their research hinges on the idea that the methods used were able to reliably measure positive and negative sentiment and neutrality in tweets. Recalling the discussion in the previous chapter of the limitations of sentiment meters, anyone making a claim based on these must demonstrate that they have a tool that gives a valid measure of Twitter opinion. Mitchell to the authors claims that their sentiment meter is 90% reliable. To demonstrate this they verify a sample of machine classification

Table 7.3 Story-lines of the thematic PCC tweets coded other

1 person more accountable than a group?	Chief constable alone	Don't really want one	Less representative	Other peoples concern	Stinker
2016 street cleaner elections	Cost	Double standard on union ballot turnouts	Little Adolfs	Pointless	Stop UKIP
3 beat officers instead	Dangerous	Feather their nests	Low profile in media	Prefer referendum	Stupid US idea
Acceptable not to vote on this occasion	Democracy in action	Forced on the public	No to PCC not an option	Privatisation of police	The election nobody talking about
Affront to democracy	Devil and deep blue sea choice	Give it a chance	Nobody gives a shit	Rotten idea	Tory diktat
Alien v Predator – we all lose	Didn't ask for this	Give us choice to elect a mayor	Nobody understands or cares	Sceptical	Vote against idea
Bloody awful initiative	Don't agree	Grey men grey suits	Nobody voting	Shade of US elections	Vote if we wanted it
Bored polling staff	Don't agree with idea	Important	None of above	Spoil your ballot	Vote No to PCC
Can't be bothered	Don't know what to do	Jobs for the boys	Not wanted	Voting not endorsement	Vote of protest

against human coding. One of the case examples in Mitchell and Hitlin's (2013) work focuses on a comparison of tweets about Obama and surveyed public opinion about him. However, with a dataset of 13 million items, it would be useful for the authors to reveal what proportion of this machine classified dataset was verified with human coding.

A practical response to those who view Twitter data as unsuitably narrow for the understanding of public opinion is that, in order to comprehensively sample the concourse of debate around a policy idea, it is necessary to sample from other social media platforms (Facebook, Tumblr, YouTube comments) or user-generated content on mainstream media sites and political blogs. In order to explore how thematic data can help compare the comprehensiveness of sources, a study of the health policy idea Compassionate Care was conducted. Following recent enquiries and the publication of the Francis Report into poor care standards at Stafford Hospital in the English Midlands (Francis, 2013), in March 2013 the Minister for Health announced a series of proposals for the NHS under the banner of the new policy idea of 'Compassionate Care'. One of the proposals was that all nurses should spend a significant period working as health care assistants (HCAs) during their training. The debate resurfaced just ahead of the annual nursing conference in April 2013. The prime minister defended the proposal, which in turn generated discussion on both mainstream and social media platforms. Several national newspapers ran comment-enabled articles on the story: on 24th April, the broadsheet newspapers *The Telegraph, The Independent* and *The Guardian* and the tabloid *Daily Mail* all covered the story and invited reader comments on their webpages. Additionally the two main newspapers for the nursing profession, *Nursing Times* and *Nursing Standard*, both invited comments on their Facebook pages. The professional body for nurses in the UK, the Royal College of Nursing (RCN), also had an active Facebook site, offering a space for members to comment on the proposals. The proposal was also discussed on Twitter.

This analysis set out to draw in comments on the likely effects of this policy on future cohorts of student nurses and compare the balance of themes across four newspapers, three Facebook pages and Twitter (see p. 159). Six coders were recruited and briefed at a workshop. Unlike the coding of PCC theme where coders were connected by an internet connection, for this study all coders were in the same room. Although working on separate machines it was possible for coders to discuss choices, share advice and agree terms. Three rounds of coding were undertaken: verification (is this related to the topic?), opinion (is this expressing an opinion?) and theme (what theme is the evoking?). Each source-based dataset was allocated to two coders for each round.

In order to determine themes for the third round of coding, each of the six coders were randomly allocated a set of 50 items, and were able to create new codes. Each new code created by a coder also appeared on the screen of their colleagues. By the end of the process, 31 codes had been created. The group of coders sat around a large screen and worked to consolidate their codes into a discrete thematic codeset. The authors of the suggested codes defined their wording and defended their decisions. The process concluded with nine substantive codes and two additional codes ('other' and 'not opinion'). The new codeset was trialled on a further set of items while still working in a group. The discussion of the codes and the choices helped to define and refine the emerging codeset. There was a clear benefit from being together in the room for this part of the process. A definition for each code was recorded and then coders were allocated different portions of the dataset, with every item being coded independently by two coders. As with the PCC thematic coding described above, the coder agreement varied by theme. For some codes the agreement was perfect or near-perfect, while for others it was considerably weaker.

Figure 7.2 shows the proportion of themes mentioned across the eight sources sampled. The *Daily Mail* and *The Telegraph*'s comments were broadly supportive of the policy idea. This support is reflected in the proportion of comments coded as 'good idea' and 'required response'. The *Nursing Standard* also had supportive comments. Although the *Daily Mail* and *The Telegraph* have fewer comments coded as broadly a 'bad idea', like other sources, there were some comments coded as 'politicisation' and 'not the answer'. *Nursing Times* and RCN both included the theme of 'risk to profession', with many of these relating to concerns about recruitment or reputation. The code 'implementation worries' was more focused on the capacity of organisations implementing the policy idea, and featured across all sources aside from the *Daily Mail* and *The Telegraph*. Both the *Nursing Times* and RCN Facebook pages contained themes uncommon in the newspapers, many of which referred to specific concerns or comments expressed between professionals rather than across wider public discourse.

The 'Apply to Others' code was a very specific and frequently occurring story-line that acquired a meme-like presence across all of the platforms. It argued that if nurses were expected to work as HCAs, so should managers, doctors, politicians or other professionals. In some instances this view was expressed by those thinking it was a good idea,

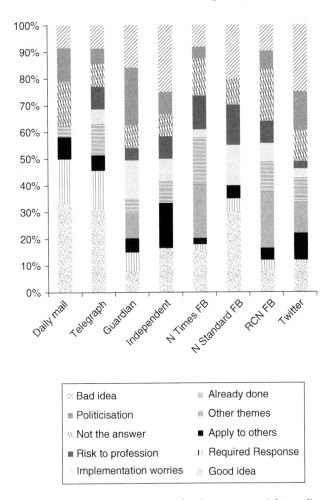

Figure 7.2 Compassionate care comments by theme across eight media sources

while in others it was expressed to convey perceived hypocrisy among the politicians advocating Compassionate Care.

This exercise reveals that Twitter can offer comprehensive coverage of current issues. The Twitter discussion of the Compassionate Care policy idea included themes popular in both the right wing and left wing newspapers, but, unlike some of the newspapers, it also included specialist discussion such as that found on the professional Facebook pages. It also contained more of the 'apply to others' themed items relative to most other sources. Although comprehensive, it is by no means balanced, with more of the tweets critical of the proposal than supportive. The findings push us to go beyond a focus on people tweeting their own views and instead focus on the influence of the mainstream media they read: this analysis of Compassionate Care revealed the capacity of newspapers, broadcasters and government agencies to mobilise their vast followerships to engage with themes and hashtags of their choosing. But it also revealed how, although its socio-demographic profile might be unbalanced, the range of sources it mediates is bewilderingly vast.

Approach 3: Crowdsourcing viewpoints

A third use for thematically coded social media data is to revisit the technique used back in Chapter 4, where Q methodology was used to explore the emerging subjectivity surrounding a recent policy idea. To recap, in Chapter 4 the technique was to sample the 'concourse of debate' surrounding a policy idea, to create a discrete set of statements, and then to invite policy actors to sort these statements into order of preference. This standardised sorting makes it possible to correlate and factorise the respondents' sorts, thereby revealing the emergence of shared viewpoints. Chapter 4 concluded by suggesting a need for Q methodology to expand its notion of concourse to accommodate online discussion. The tools and techniques discussed in subsequent chapters offer some exciting possibilities for Q methodology research to be combined with text analytics.

The availability of several thousand opinions on a policy issue brings with it several data management and sampling challenges. The thematic coding and classification of user-generated comments reveals considerable repetition. It is possible, through a process of disambiguation, de-duplication and thematic classification, to systematically map the concourse of debate, but there still remains the challenge of selecting the final Q set, which is often limited to between 25 and 75 statements. In constructing the Q set there is often a temptation to over-elaborate the process, to try and choose the most diverse items from those available. There is no perfect Q set, but there are good ones. A good Q set includes both divergent and mainstream arguments. The solution proposed in most studies is some form of balanced block. This entails drawing up a two dimensional sampling grid, with a range of themes along one dimension and a spectrum of debate along the other – Left/Right, republican/democrat, liberal/authoritarian, for/against.

The case described below involves a change to housing finance for those in receipt of housing benefit in England. The Coalition

Government policy sought to end what it called the 'Spare room subsidy': housing benefit recipients who had one or more spare rooms in their property should be deemed to be under-occupying and from April 2013 they should pay for the spare room out of their own pocket and not be subsidised by the public purse. In real terms this amounted to a reduction in benefits, with tenants required to make up the shortfall or move to a smaller, cheaper property. For those opposed to the policy, it soon became known as the 'Bedroom Tax'.

The label Bedroom Tax was first mentioned in the media in December 2011 when the National Housing Federation published a report describing the proposed idea as 'essentially a bedroom tax' (National Housing Federation, 2011). The only previous use of the term was two years earlier in 2009 when a policy idea of taxing housing extensions was described as a Bedroom Tax – an example sharing the same label, but naming a different policy. Although both labels – Bedroom Tax and Spare Room Subsidy – were in common use, analysis of social media data collected during April and May 2013 shows that the vast majority of discussion used 'Bedroom Tax'.

The study discussed here therefore explores both mentions of the Bedroom Tax and Spare Room Subsidy, and the viewpoints that developed around the initiative of reducing housing benefit for those deemed to be under-occupying; the aim of the study was to gain in-depth, qualitative insight into the different viewpoints that crystallised around this policy idea. Those opposed to the Bedroom Tax organised petitions, protests, marches and set up campaign websites, blogs and Twitter feeds. The study draws on Twitter data collected using DiscoverText and visualised using Topsy.com. The activity on Twitter averaged around 5,000 tweets per day during April and 500 per day during May. Importantly, particular events reported in the media caused dramatic daily spikes of activity; for example, on 11 May 2013, 25,000 tweets discussed a woman committing suicide and blaming the Bedroom Tax, before daily mentions returned to an equilibrium of several hundred per day. Similarly, on 30th March 43,000 tweets were recorded in one day before returning to a few thousand per day.

The study here fetched tweets over 72 hours between 8th and 11th April using DiscoverText and the Twitter API, with fetches every 15 minutes. A total of 8,155 were collected. Contrasted against Topsy.com's suggested activity, the 8,155 amounts to around 80% of the total activity. The phrases bedroom tax, #bedroomtax, spareroom subsidy and #spareroomsubsidy were chosen as keywords, and pulled in 4,122, 3,814, 201 and 18 tweets, respectively. The programme was set up so that the same tweet would not be collected in different fetches. For example if a tweet contained both Bedroom Tax and Spareroom Subsidy, it would only be collected in one fetch.

The archive was then de-duplicated using the techniques described in Chapter 6. Of the 8,155 tweets collected, 3,128 (38%) were identical retweets or quoted tweets. At a threshold of 70% duplication, the remaining 5,027 were reduced to 3,704. This de-duplicated dataset included 907 cluster seed tweets and 2,797 single items. Through a further round of de-duplication it was possible to reduce the dataset by over half to 3,704 items. A random sample of 100 items was created and coded by three people on a three way codeset of *statement, not statement, don't know*. The coding was adjudicated for validity and a kappa score of 0.61 of coder agreement was reached. The coding was used as training data to classify the 3,704 items. The dataset was split by classification at a certainty threshold of 85%. A dataset of 983 possible statements was then created and allocated to three coders with a new codeset of statement/not statement. This coding pass was then used to retrain the classifier. The set was then machine-coded by list – coding 100 at a time rather than one at a time. The resulting coding took a total of two hours of human coding time, compared to an expected total of around seven hours without the machine classifier (based on an average of seven seconds per tweet).

A sample of 100 statements was then extracted and iteratively coded for themes. This created ten themes, consolidated from an initial set of 19. The ten codes were split broadly for and against, although some overlapped; for example, there were statements that supported the idea of ending the Spare Room Subsidy but thought the policy was poorly implemented by the current government. The 100 tweets were allocated to one of the ten themes. Duplicate arguments were removed and language was adjusted to translate the sentiment and story-line of the tweet into a statement for a Q study. The final list of 25 statements was selected, with attempts to broadly balance the tweets between those for and against (12 and 13), with some flexibility to ensure the diversity of the debate was covered. The statements were piloted with five respondents, and based on feedback, the wording of one of the statements was modified. In total, 26 sorts were collected between 13th April and 26th April in 2013.

A fuller account of how the statements were administered and interpretation of the viewpoints can be found in Jeffares (2014). In summary, the Q sorts were collected using POETQ (Jeffares et al., 2011) and on a dedicated project website. Respondents were recruited primarily through Twitter and Facebook advertisements. The three emergent viewpoints are outlined in brief below.

Viewpoint 1: Lack of supply, nowhere to go, no choice

This viewpoint argues that there isn't enough social housing into which people can move and the government have done this without making provision.

> It isn't a choice for most of these people as there isn't enough places for them to move to.
>
> (YST Home Owner, M.)

> They [the Government] have sold off social housing to landlords who charge exorbitant rents that councils will not then pay. Related to somebody affected.

Viewpoint 2: Good policy mired by myth and hypocrisy

This viewpoint argues that the Spare Room Subsidy is a good policy idea which is being undermined by the hypocrisy of 'socialists' refusing to downgrade to help out others who need the space (s16, –1,3,–3). This viewpoint argues that the Bedroom Tax campaign is riddled with misinformation and that claims of a rise in homelessness resulting from the policy are exaggerated:

> Firstly it is not a tax, and secondly it makes little sense to assume this will lead to homelessness, it is not a removal of housing benefit, just a reduction in certain cases.
>
> (Private sector employee)

> My in-laws downsized from their family sized council home and were much happier in a smaller easier to manage home. It is hard to sort out the fact and the fiction.
>
> (Parent & Home Owner)

Viewpoint 3: Lacks clarity, poor idea.

This viewpoint argues that it is not a tax but that doesn't make it a good idea – it will harm vulnerable members of the community, and those that instigated it should look first to their own use of money

I really struggle to see how this is going to work in practice. It feels like a 'good on paper – rubbish in reality' policy to me.

(Student, Home Owner)

[The view that *People in council houses should count themselves lucky for the cheap rent they pay in the first place]* 'left me feeling very uncomfortable...as someone who has family living in a Council flat, and knowing how much they struggle, this condescending statement left me feeling annoyed'.

(Student, Home Owner)

The viewpoints here are 'operant' – rather than being based on theoretical connections between statements, they emerge empirically from the sorting exercises conducted by respondents. Rather than see the factor solution as the endpoint, it could be used to inform further work. The group of viewpoints resulting from the Q sorting draws equivalence around sets of statements. The distinguishing statements, and the story-lines contained, offer a means to train a classifier. The search would identify possible items from a large dataset. The factors could also be used to create a codebook and train human coders to code for viewpoints.

Conclusion

This chapter has explored the challenge of coding opinion in social media data. It has explored the potential of combining human coding and machine classification. The approaches developed here offer an alternative to the automated sentiment meters introduced in Chapter 6. The approaches described acknowledge that user-generated content comes from a range of sources, where duplication is inevitable, and near-duplication hidden. It also argues that while machine classification is possible, it works best when trained by human coding.

The object of study in this chapter, and the whole book, has been to interpret policy ideas. These are by definition recently coined and variably understood. Particular events, scandals, launches, speeches, broadcasts and the like all help to promote fluctuating amounts of activity on social media platforms. The example of the PCC election and its build-up saw a growing interest in this policy idea, with a violent spike in activity around the day of the election and particularly the morning of the results.

The focus of this chapter is less concerned with the simple frequency of activity, but rather the way in which social media is used to critique or promote policy ideas, and the way in which it reflects the arrival and departure of certain themes. These themes are demands attached by actors to the meaning or definition of the policy idea.

Using the PCC election as an example and drawing on an archive of Twitter data, the first task was therefore to isolate opinions from other kinds of tweets; many are conversations, promotional broadcasts or opportunist spam. Through a process of coding, working with a team of coders, it was possible to train a machine classifier to distinguish opinionated tweets. These opinionated tweets could then be iteratively coded for themes. The five most prominent themes could then be tracked over the three week period building up to the election. The fluctuating volume of certain tweets on certain days is of some interest, but is not the main aim or claim of the research process. Rather, what is most interesting in terms of understanding the evolution of policy ideas is how themes are reiterated daily.

The act of tweeting an opinion about a policy idea and drawing on a common theme cannot be taken for granted. Each tweet in isolation is of negligible importance. Yes, it is possible for an influential user of Twitter to strike a chord and be retweeted. But their influence is grounded in conformity. Their conscious or unconscious capacity to identify a theme and express this succinctly has the potential to be disruptive, but it is mostly about conforming to an establishing norm. The challenge facing public policy research is that the emergence and disappearance of themes takes place in time frames that are difficult to capture. While the example of the PCC over a three week period is long enough to identify the emergence of arguments around *shambolic organisation, lack of information, politicisation,* those other short-lived themes – those that arise around issues that last barely 24 hours – are less easy to spot without systematic capture and analysis.

The chapter concluded with two further suggestions of how thematic classification can be applied in order to interpret a policy idea. One suggestion responded to the critique that particular sources, such as Twitter, are biased towards particular arguments and lack comprehensiveness. The example explored eight sources of user-generated content around one single policy idea. While it was by no means a conclusive study of this, it demonstrated how Twitter might have political bias, in this case against the Conservative Government policy, but it also contained a comprehensive set of themes broadly found elsewhere. In part this can be explained by acknowledging the degree to which these platforms are increasingly integrated. Content posted on one platform is posted and shared elsewhere on other platforms. Furthermore, those that comment on online newspaper articles are not just readers of that paper, but also often antagonists looking for an argument with their subjective sparring partners. Overall, what this approach offers is a means of benchmarking themes attached to the policy idea at particular critical moments in its lifecycle.

The final suggestion for applying the thematic classifier is to employ Q methodology in order to identify viewpoints. Viewpoints were defined in Chapter 4 as shared perspectives on a particular policy idea, and informed by correlating the standardised preferences of a diverse group of respondents. The example sampled the concourse of debate surrounding a policy idea and drew out key story-lines in preparation for a Q study, which revealed distinct viewpoints around the policy. As well as being interesting findings in themselves, these viewpoints offer the potential to create defined searches and ultimately codesets that could identify the presence of these viewpoints in large archives.

The use of Q in this way takes us beyond just identifying themes, to suggesting which themes are central to a particular viewpoint and how they are interrelated. Other tools suggest something similar, such as Leximancer (Angus et al., 2013) but these rely on frequencies and colocations rather than the trained judgement of human coders informing, in turn, Bayesian classifiers.

We are some way from complete automation. Classifiers can perform analyses quicker and, potentially, as accurately as humans, but this does not mean we can be free of doubt. In the process of developing codesets in teams, unexpected differences of opinion lead to discussion and revision, and agreement can be improved but will never be 100%.

8
The Future of Hashtag Politics

Policy ideas have at least five characteristics: they are ideational, instrumental, visionary, container-like and branded. Policy ideas are also mortal; they have a distinguishable lifecycle, but one that is difficult to measure. While some analyses focus on activity, in terms of how much is being said, another approach is to focus on what proportion of the population have heard of the idea or use it in everyday speech. In both cases we are looking for signs of demise, of activity reducing or attention shifting elsewhere. Alternatively, we can focus on expectation or the accumulation of meaning. Here we are looking for signs of inflated expectations or disillusionment, or in case of the latter, overloaded and nebulous concepts. Meaning is carried over from one policy idea to the next, but ultimately, in its entirety, a policy idea is officially dead when its name is no longer mentioned, when the circus moves on.

Knowing if a policy idea is 'dead' matters because as policy actors – as policy-maker, collaborator, analyst or citizen – we invest in policy ideas, be they our own or those of others. Many public servants will recall a time when they edited a PowerPoint slide in a presentation to fit with the idea of the day. Many in the charity or academic sectors will recall bidding for money, couching their application in the lingua franca of the funding council. Many a senior public official will recall the moment when they began to doubt if their initiative was worth pursuing, whether to defend it to the media, whether to attempt a re-launch. Many of these actors will recall being invited to the launch of a new initiative, or hearing of the latest report, the press release, the workshop, the associated activity, the surrounding enthusiasm. We remember the launch of a policy idea but we seldom acknowledge its passing.

All of this discussion of policy ideas and their lives and deaths is given further focus by the competition for attention, the rapid speed of communication and the multiple channels by which we communicate and receive news and information. In this digital era, the evidence suggests that it is unlikely that any policy idea can be sustained for more than 1,000 days. It is difficult to know whether or not this digital era exacerbates the demise of policy ideas and shortens their lifespan. For every new threat these digital communications pose, they also offer a strikingly cheap and decentralised means to communicate to a chosen public or a particular audience. What is clear is that to begin to explain how digital communication influences the lifecycles of policy ideas requires policy analysts to harness new sources of data and methods of analysis.

Although from a very different era, Lasswell's 1949 definition of key symbols remains one of the most helpful definitions of policy ideas. This definition of policy ideas as 'a terse string of words that gain meaning by repetition and context' (Lasswell, 1949), offers a dynamic definition as something for which, although the label may be static, a range of meanings circulate, crystallise and accumulate. Similarly, applying discourse theory to policy ideas, such as Birmingham's Flourishing Neighbourhoods policy, offers a theoretical means to comprehend such accumulation and overloading of meaning. Methods such as Q methodology, that combine qualitative and quantitative techniques, are helpful when applied to policy ideas like Total Place and Bedroom Tax to demonstrate how the viewpoints can be identified by comparing Q sorts.

Q methodology also lends us Stephenson's notion of concourse, focusing our attention on the idea that surrounding every topic is a dynamic but bounded set of arguments. The starting point for a Q study is for researchers to immerse themselves in this concourse, and develop a means to methodically sample its diversity. These techniques were honed in the 20th century, where concourse was drawn from interviews, documents and print media; these techniques were first developed in an off-line world. While Q methodology remains vital, the techniques must adapt to the challenge of sampling online concourses.

Asking questions about policy ideas reveals the practice of hashtag politics – the practice of purposefully creating or engaging with discrete brand-like policy ideas. The hashtag is a metaphor for something broader. On social media platforms hashtags are analogous to policy ideas. They bracket ideas, serve as instruments, convey visions and, perhaps most importantly, offer a container for others to add alternative meanings and associations. Hashtags are brand-like, offering unique identifiers that make them searchable for users of social media platforms. In the policy sphere when policy actors coin a policy idea, they do so with the same rationale in mind. They seek to accommodate a range of policy proposals and initiatives and package these in a form understandable to a wider audience. The clear advantage of this is that it offers a brand to nurture, but at the same time it creates a space for contestation, where new demands can be added and meaning can accumulate. This reveals the limitations of the agency of policy actors to control the meaning and reception of their pet projects. Therefore hashtag politics is not only the coining of policy ideas but also a battle for control.

It is easy to understand why hashtag politics might be construed as something new, made possible by the arrival of digital communications and social media platforms. Rather than something new, however, it would be more appropriate to frame hashtag politics as a practice that is becoming increasingly common, and whose role is simply made more explicit by the digital trace of online text and developments in interpretive text analytics. Flourishing Neighbourhoods and the practices that brought this policy idea to bear on city of Birmingham in the early 2000s is a case in point. Flourishing Neighbourhoods pre-dated social media and the practice of using hashtags by several years, but the intention of the policy actors who coined and fostered it are clear. For city leaders at the time it served as a means to articulate a range of measures and ultimately to maintain control of an environment in which their autonomy was potentially being hollowed out and fragmented, in which budgets were being centralised and a trajectory of working across boundaries in new hybrid forms of governance was emerging (Skelcher et al., 2013).

Relatedly, hashtag politics is more than an expression of the mediatisation of policy-making, it is more than an exercise in communications. Communications matter at the sharp end of coining and first launching new policy ideas, but the practice of hashtag politics is more than this. To reduce hashtag politics in order to equate with the increased use of spin doctors or communication advisors, soundbites or slogans would be to down play its significance as an integral practice of policy-making and fundamentally, the expression of politics

Policy actors have had to adapt to changes in how news is made and disseminated, and the fragmentation of media channels. The Big Society was one policy idea that stood out because it was heavily promoted and branded, launched and re-launched. But not all policy ideas are quite as big. One of the developments of hashtag politics is that the cost of coining and launching and fostering a policy idea is decreasing.

Here the mantra of Silicon Valley comes into play: Fail fast, fail early, fail cheaply. The next phase of hashtag politics will find policy-makers experimenting with ideas and intuitively backing those with greatest potential.

It matters that policy ideas be unique. Hashtag politics involves the creation of unique names that are searchable, traceable, and can be distinguished from the others. We see from the examples in this book that the labels for policy ideas can come from the top – a decision to call a policy a policy – but also from open public discussion. The 'Bedroom Tax' is a case in point, as an example of a popular or organic label that arose from public discussion.

Hashtag politics is as much about creating as it is about forgetting. There is a curious temporality of policy ideas in that they can be heavily promoted, trailed, discussed, and then so easily forgotten. Focusing on policy as a process of equivalence draws on a theoretical account of how meaning accumulates, and offers the means to track the accumulation of meaning over time – to track a policy idea on its journey from a particular meaning to dislocation.

The focus on accumulated meaning also highlights a preoccupation with counting. We are still in the habit of counting citations, or counting the number of times a word is mentioned in a party leader's speech. To be sure, this gives us a broad picture; just as counting mentions of a policy idea in newspapers remains something worth doing – for example, tracking the frequency of mentions of the Big Society showed that this policy idea was on the wane. This brings us back to the question of what to count – mentions, activity, adoption or, for that matter, expectation. We need to think about equivalence or, put another way, a measurement of modification – of how far from its original meaning the policy idea has strayed.

The short-term nature of these ideas may make us reluctant to invest in their conceptual development. However, the policy idea is a useful category as it situates us somewhere between specific programmes and broader, abstract notions such as freedom or democracy. So while there are fads and fashions around the use of terms like 'leadership', 'transformation' or 'innovation', these are not in the same category and should not be confused with policy ideas like the Big Society. Similarly, policy ideas must not be confused with specific programmes of action – the types of programmes that Berman argues are too narrow to be interesting. What we have seen in this book is how policy ideas can take on a life of their own, and how the original sponsors often cannot retain control of the meaning of their pet project.

The spread of smart phones will increase and an ever greater percentage of the population will have the technical potential to engage with and contribute to debates about policy. What will characterise this era is ever greater volumes of communication, and therefore increased use of strategies to punctuate and bracket discussion. It will require new skills, some assisted by technology, but overall, those that will succeed are those with an intuition of when to invest resources and when to move on. This cannot be the preserve of elites. It will entail the wider use of tools to visualise the rise and demise of policy ideas, to track trends, expectations and adoption, to identify the influencers, and so on. The migration of hashtag politics as a practice from off-line to online democratises the process. Many more tools will be developed in future years that will make interpreting the landscape of policy-making as intuitive as a Google search. The future of hashtag politics will free up policy-makers to attempt many more policy ideas than previously, with increased insight about when to abandon an idea and move on to something else. This fail fast, fail early approach will in turn create considerable challenges for policy analysis to adapt to new patterns of practice.

Put simply, it is not enough to focus on the big ideas – the New Deals, the Big Societies. The shifting patterns towards hashtag politics will mean policies will come and go unnoticed by the political historians. For policy analysis not to adapt to this would be to miss out on a huge portion of what is occurring. The policy ideas that survive 1,000 hours deserve as much attention as those that last 1,000 days. And we can only begin to give them this attention if we adapt our techniques to be able to map the response. This goes further than issuing an opinion poll: it requires the identification of the emergence of viewpoints by capturing digital discussion and adopting systematic methods such as Q methodology and Online Text Analytics. Policy analysis is well placed to explain this new chapter for public policy-making, but it will require the acquisition of new skills and adaptation and development of techniques to do so.

Implications

There are a variety of implications for different communities of identity mentioned through the course of this book. This section will consider some of the implications for each of these readerships.

The first set of implications is for policy actors. The policy actors featured in this book included the neighbourhood activists involved in Flourishing Neighbourhoods, whose original idea was subverted; the city councillors who chose Flourishing Neighbourhoods as a key theme; and the many practitioners who later attached their projects to the policy idea. We saw those engaged with the Big Society variably categorising what they thought it was, and their annoyance that it was ill-defined. We saw with Total Place how professionals working on the pilot project had developed a set of viewpoints around what they thought it meant. In all three cases came the suggestion that these policy ideas were dead after 1,000 days. The latter chapters covered the Home Office-led social media campaign around MyPCC, and how this was quickly overtaken in terms of volume by more organic descriptions. We saw how opportunities were taken to broadcast and publicise, but how engaging the support of influential users, such as the prime minister, opened up the opportunity for critique and derision. We saw too how attempts at tagging policy with labels such as 'Spare Room Subsidy' or 'Compassionate Care' will not necessarily demarcate where the debate takes place. There is not a single platform or hashtag that all will use.

To policy actors

So what are the implications of this research for policy practice? First, it must be acknowledged that policy ideas are now an established and core aspect of policy-making. In the battle to disseminate a message that can compete in an environment of multiple channels and information overload, the creation of effective labels for policy ideas is part of the craft of policy-making. Second, accept that vagueness is part of the appeal; the container-like qualities are what draw people to an idea and allow them the important opportunity to attach meaning and demands. Nebulousness underpins the appeal of a policy idea. Third, accept that the agency of original sponsors will be challenged. Accept that organic labels, hashtags and alternate meanings will arise. Fourth, it is important listen. Invest modest resources in social media monitoring software, but it is more important to train policy researchers to integrate new forms of data into their research work. Following one hashtag or set of users is not enough. But at the same time, do not rely on automated analytics alone, such as sentiment monitors, when making decisions. Five, avoid the temptation only to chase large followerships and to broadcast; take time to engage, as commercial companies do. Six, although riots and uprisings are sometimes attributed to social media, it is important to acknowledge for now that mainstream media remains the main protagonist of activity related to policy. Acknowledge, however, that attachment to policy ideas is gradual, cumulative and eventually disruptive. Acknowledge when the policy idea is entering its final stages, be prepared to disinvest and do not mislead your collaborators.

To social media analysts

Another stakeholder community found in this book is the social media analysts – scholars, consultants and prolific tweeters. We heard of them first in Chapter 5, in which it was highlighted that, since 2010, there has been something of a Gold Rush in terms of accepted standards of analysis, about the basis of claims, about what constitutes good and bad research. The four characterisations of social media analysis described four distinctive motivations to develop this work. The economic or commercial imperative is driving much of the flurry of activity online, characterised by social media marketing, LinkedIn groups, and high hopes for software. Close behind is work about social movements, a social media sociology, along with political researchers excited by opportunities to predict turnout or election results. Most fragmented is a fourth category of professional practice. There is a sense that social media and associated technologies are reshaping professional practice, from research to law and order, health care to journalism. Connected to this is a question of data, about who owns them, and whether they are accessed or captured, at what price and with what safeguards.

What are the implications of this book for this growing, ambitious and fragmented community of data analysts? First is to say that the main focus of this book has been policy ideas rather than a comprehensive guide to the future of social media analytics. That said, cases like Total Place and Flourishing Neighbourhoods put into perspective that the life and death of hashtag politics is by no means brand new, but through social media analytics it can be better understood. Second, while the industry must continue to strive for standards, those cultivating this new stream of computational social science research must acknowledge that there is no need to completely rewrite the rules of ethics and research. Yes, data can be high volume and high velocity, and not always immediately available in machine readable format, but the basic processes and expectations of social science research remain. In the clamour and excitement about big data, GIS mapping and network analysis focus on the metadata, and neglect unstructured user-generated text. In response to this, interpretive research has much to offer. Third, multiple platform data and access to the 'full firehose' of data is desirable but not always essential, and the legitimacy of the research depends not on the price of data but rather on the fit with research design, with the questions being asked and the claims being made. To dismiss work because it stems from a single platform or draws on a sample, without consideration of the research objective, is short sighted. For example, Twitter might not be representative demographically speaking, but it can easily be comprehensive in terms of the concourse of a debate. If the aim is to sample the diversity of opinion then, as opinion pollsters find when working with people, a sample will more than suffice. Fourth, we are probably at a point of transition where creating the user-generated content has never been cheaper and easier, where the Library of Congress archive of tweets increases by half a billion a day, and yet, while we have the technology to store it, we lack the capability, the will, to make it freely available. Until that time, social and computer scientists should resist the commercial temptation to obscure their techniques behind commercial pay-walls and opaque algorithms, and in doing so hiding the limitations of their sentiment meters. Unless this is opened up, the future will see only a small elite having historic access to social media data and the tools to make sense of it.

To public policy researchers and policy analysts

The third community present in this book are those that conduct policy analysis and policy evaluation; broadly, public policy researchers. The work of public policy researchers was featured in the opening chapters, in defining policy ideas as ideas, as policy instruments, visions, containers and brands. We heard from the political theorists behind political discourse theory and interpretive scholars advocating the role of story-lines; and Q methodologists interested in the scientific study of subjectivity around policy also featured.

What are the implications of this book for public policy research? The first point goes to those who see lesser value in high- or middle-level ideas over specific policy initiatives (Berman, 2009). Public policy needs to revisit and acknowledge how thousand day policy ideas are part of everyday policy-making, and that distinct subjective viewpoints crystallise around these. Second, it is important to acknowledge that although the use of unique identifiers and tagging makes these policies easier to search, trace and monitor, the discussion takes place across a broad range of platforms and locations, where discussion is periodic and posts may often last only 24 hours. Policy researchers should be wary of reading too much into specific hashtags or the quantity of retweets, and aim to understand the nuanced practice of subversion.

Third, commercial colleagues are leading the way but it should also be acknowledged that the work of political psephologists is a different project than interpreting the implementation of policy ideas. This latter remains underdeveloped and presents a great opportunity for policy scholars to reignite the study of ideas in the policy process. Fourth, it is easy to fall back on familiar metrics of frequency, the rise and fall of agendas, diffusion or expectation; however, it is important to acknowledge equivalence and accumulation. Meaning changes over time. It is nuanced, difficult to identify, but vitally important and therefore should be part of the repertoire of policy research. Fifth, influencers and disruptive, punctuated moments do sometimes matter, but not in all cases. Arab Springs and London Riots are the exceptions. Focus only on exceptional cases and we will miss the everyday, gradual accumulation and reiteration of themes that culminate in a dramatic but easily overlooked dislocation of meaning. Sixth, we need not be divided by data. These data are a treasure equally for multilevel modelling and in-depth text analysis, for corpus linguists and ethnographers, and so on. The task is to make these data accessible and to promote the development and accessibility of the tools required for analysis.

To Q methodologists

In addition to policy analysis more generally, this book has featured the arguments and work of specific areas of the academy, namely Q methodology studies and interpretive policy studies. There are conclusions for them too. The applications of Q methodology to the policy ideas of Total Place and Compassionate Care demonstrated the value of systematically sampling, sorting and correlating the discussion surrounding policy ideas as a means of revealing shared viewpoints. In the case of Total Place the method demonstrated how viewpoints crystallise around emergent policies. In the case of Compassionate Care, we explored how high volume high velocity discussion surrounding a current issue could be sampled and sorted by respondents. The approach to research design matched the choice of data. High velocity data were in turn met by a smaller than average Q set and administered online. The approach used for Compassionate Care revealed how Q need not involve months of sampling and careful preparation to be meaningful and valid. Furthermore, rather than viewing the discovery of viewpoints as an endpoint or final result, as is so common in Q research, the viewpoints revealed can be integrated into further coding and analysis. Rather than viewing the cases as 64 or 28 'respondents', in the context of the overall approach of this book, it would be better framed as 63 or 28 crowdsourced 'participants-as-analysts' contributing to the development of codebooks. We remain some way off developing a means of developing Q sets with a single click of a mouse, but with the techniques developed above, we are somewhat closer. In a world where user-generated content is proliferating, the long-established technique of Q has a great deal to offer, but it must adapt to be able to sample high volume and high velocity discussion.

To interpretive policy researchers

As high profile court cases have shown, interpreting the meaning or intent of something as short as an individual tweet is by no means simple. The easy way out is to write off short message data as something only for quantification. It is why most research using Twitter data, for example, focuses on the metadata rather than the richness of the discussion contained in the tweets. Early attempts to code opinion in the PCC case revealed that achieving high levels of inter-coder agreement is problematic. Improvement comes in part from providing research teams with improved definitions and clearer examples. But the turning point in coding PCC tweets came from focusing on story-lines, our definition drawn from the earlier work of Maarten Hajer (Hajer, 1995, p. 68, 2009). We discovered how most opinionated tweets, no matter how short, contain crisp generative story-lines directed towards the policy. It is these that carry and project the meaning towards the tweet. The task is not one of assuming that the author of the tweet is endorsing the sentiment of the story-line; by quoting or retweeting it, their sentiment towards it at that very moment is somewhat secondary. Instead Kaplan and Haenlein's (2010) point about the role of social media platforms offering 'ambient awareness' matters here, in that the mention of the story-line is a form of subscription or reiteration of that story-line. It is this that is adding to the gradual accumulation of meaning as depicted in the stacked area graph in Figure 7.1.

Although interpretive policy studies offer much in terms of understanding the 'social life' of policy ideas, so much interpretive policy work relies on the judgement of solitary researchers and complex hierarchical codesets. The use of DiscoverText in chapters 6 and 7 highlights an opportunity for interpretive research to explore the potential of crowdsourcing coding tasks, a focus on short and simple codesets, the need for building in checks for coder agreement and adjudicating validity. Interpretive researchers sometimes question whether terms such as reliability and validity belong in their lexicon. It is best expressed in a call for approaches to interpretive research that are systematic, transparent and credible, and this starts by using tools that can assist with simple checks to see if everybody in the research term shares a working definition of a code.

There are three instances in this book where human judgement has been surrendered, as it were, to the machine. In the two Q studies mentioned, Total Place and Compassionate Care, the responses were submitted to correlation and factorisation, and this guided the interpretation of viewpoints. In the PCC case the human coding informed the machine classification that suggested how further coding should proceed. These approaches represent both a threat and an opportunity to interpretive research. The threat comes from an assumption that interpretive insight can be gained with less need for face-to-face interviews or observation. The worry here is that such mechanisation of the interpretive process is short-circuiting important insight and empathy. Viewpoints are tacit and therefore the loss of insight is intangible but nevertheless worrisome. But social science cannot afford to miss this opportunity. Availability of research grants for interpretive research might be one consideration, but moreover the high volume high velocity nature of user-generated content online signals a need to adapt interpretive techniques for an era of digital data.

Hashtag politics is a practice of modern policy-making where policy ideas are coined, fostered and imbued with meaning and associations, before eventually being overlooked, forgotten and seldom mentioned again. Speculating about whether a policy idea is doomed, or old wine in new bottles, or indeed 'dead', is part of a political process, but is not a clear certification of death. Rather, it is mentions and associations that sustain a policy idea. This activity fluctuates daily, often prompted by events or outputs. The arguments and themes attached to a policy idea are a combination of previous story-lines and some new ones. Policy ideas die when people no longer speak of them. However, some arguments will live on, and our ability to uncover these processes will come from further development of systematic, transparent and credible interpretive methods.

The practice of hashtag politics has evolved in response to an increasingly congested and mediatised environment, where the recent and rapid growth of high speed internet connections, smart phones and social media has brought with it the potential to extend or curtail the life of a policy idea. For policy actors and analysts alike, understanding hashtag politics requires intuition aided by innovation, in terms of how the sourcing and analysis of data can go beyond simply monitoring fluctuations or crude sentiment. Understanding hashtag politics requires interpretive insight and an understanding of how meaning, story-lines and viewpoints accumulate. The policy ideas propagated by hashtag politics might last between a thousand hours and a thousand days, but as a policy practice, hashtag politics has a long and rich future ahead.

9
Appendix

Chapter 3 Comparison of two policy ideas over 1,000 days

Table 9.1 Comparing the 1,000-day lifecycle of Flourishing Neighbourhoods and the Big Society

	Flourishing Neighbourhoods	Big Society
Conceived	2000 – Community activist description for sustainable neighbourhoods development – picked up by consultants advising city leaders to define their urban renaissance policy	Credited to Steve Hilton, David Cameron's chief policy advisor/director of strategy
	Became key theme for major policy conference 'Highbury 3' in February 2001	
Birth announcements	5 February 2002	11 November 2009
	Flourishing Neighbourhoods named as one of three strategic priorities – 'The city centre has a spring in its step and this sense of confidence and pride must reappear in all the city neighbourhoods' (BCC Cabinet Statement 2002, in Dale, 2002, p. 3)	Formally launched in July 2010, although first mentioned by David Cameron as leader of the opposition delivering the 2009 Hugo Young memorial lecture, 11th November
	Highbury 3 conference, Conference summary document – newspaper articles, strategy documents, working group	Widespread use of blogs and Twitter hashtag

148

Table 9.1   (Continued)

	Flourishing Neighbourhoods	Big Society
Lifecycle – how discussed	Three years – Initial excitement particularly among voluntary and community sector	Discussed online through Facebook, Twitter
Forgetting	Local Labour group decision to include flourishing neighbourhoods as a campaign slogan politicised the brand; incoming coalition administration announced alternative 'vibrant villages' policy	
Death notice	2 October 2004 *Birmingham Post*: 'Sir Albert Bore, former council boss and leader of the Labour group, had much to say for himself at last Monday's cabinet'... Why, he demanded, had the coalition scrapped the appellation 'Flourishing Neighbourhoods' when referring to the Birmingham suburbs in favour of 'vibrant urban villages'?... By airbrushing out Flourishing Neighbourhoods and adopting vibrant urban villages the coalition was, said Sir Albert... 'calling a Dalmatian a black and white spotted mongrel' (Dale, 2004)	16 April 2012 *The Daily Telegraph*: 'The Big Society theme is now, in effect, dead – its corpse riddled with bullets fired by a jealous government machine that had no intention of relinquishing any power' (Nelson, 2012) Also 3 March 2012, Mirror on Sunday: 'Voluntary groups say David Cameron's "Big Society" is dead in the water – just as the idea's inventor Steve Hilton quits No10 for a year-long teaching sabbatical in the Californian sun' (Moss & Anderson, 2012).
Lifespan	5.2.02 to 2.10.04 (970 days). 31 months	11.11.09 to 16.4.12 (887 days). 29 months

Table 9.2 Total Place statements and factor arrays

		1	2	3	4
1	Total Place is a single public sector budget for [the area]	−1	2	2	0
2	Total Place equals more central control, thought up by accountants and pushed down to local authorities	−4	−4	−4	2
3	Total Place is returning to a general purpose local authority but with multiple providers	0	−2	0	−2
4	Total Place is about statutory authorities commissioning more and providing less	−2	−2	−2	1
5	Total Place is about a joint intelligence and shared analysis approach	2	3	4	0
6	Total Place needs to be driven by politicians, because left to officers or civil servants to make these changes, we'd still be talking about it in four years time	−4	−1	2	0
7	Total Place is cooperating with central government, not working against it	0	2	−1	−1
8	Total Place requires leadership to achieve whole systems change	2	4	2	4
9	Total Place starts from our knowledge rather than a blank sheet of paper	0	3	0	−2
10	Total Place is about changing the culture of organisations	3	4	2	3
11	Total Place is about taking risks	2	−1	1	2
12	Total Place means starting with a clean sheet of paper	−1	−4	−1	−1
13	Total Place is about people at the ground floor level making it happen by just doing it	1	−3	0	−4
14	Total Place is one amongst many other well-meaning ideas	−3	0	−4	1
15	Total Place is a budget driven way of thinking about the world	−1	0	−2	−1
16	Total Place is required because from 2011 we are going to run out of money	−2	0	−2	0
17	The most critical aspect of Total Place is the financial analysis	−3	0	−2	−2
18	Total Place is about a pragmatic rather than ideological approach to commissioning	1	1	−1	−2
19	Total Place is about realising cashable efficiencies by stopping activity and decommissioning services	2	−2	−3	−1
20	Total Place means we get 'more for less' from the total public money going into a locality	1	3	3	3
21	Total Place is about upstream investment to save downstream costs	0	1	0	1

Table 9.2   (Continued)

		1	2	3	4
22	Total Place is a single performance framework for local government, health and the police	−1	2	1	−2
23	Total Place will require a new statutory responsibility across all agencies to tackle issues together	−1	−1	4	4
24	Total Place is about integrated local wrap around services	2	2	0	1
25	Total Place is a shift from fixing things to stopping them breaking in the first Place	2	0	3	2
26	Total Place will create a dialogue between the voluntary and statutory sectors	0	1	1	0
27	Total Place is about focusing attention on high cost users and thereby providing an opportunity to break recurring patterns and dramatically reduce overall expenditure	−1	1	3	3
28	Total Place is about the budget allocated to one public service being spent by another public service	−2	−2	−3	−3
29	Total Place is an opportunity to promote diversity and a multicultural society	1	1	0	−3
30	Total Place is about understanding where you need to go to get help	1	−1	−1	1
31	Total Place is about giving people what they need, in the way they want it	4	−1	1	−1
32	Total Place is about addressing the whole person, not just the presenting problem	3	0	2	1
33	Total Place should be driven by an inquisitive understanding of what makes customers tick, each and everyday	3	1	1	2
34	Total Place is about managing customer expectations	0	−1	−2	−1
35	Total Place is about looking further ahead to a long timescale for change	0	2	0	0
36	Total Place will give citizens the power to decide how money is spent	0	−3	0	−4
37	Total Place is about shaping the market	−1	0	−1	1
38	Total Place is about working with local people to design and develop services	4	0	1	2
39	Total Place is about reshaping dysfunctional aspirations to fit with social norms	−3	−3	−3	−3
40	Total Place is about how we are using the skills of the voluntary and private sectors	1	1	1	0
41	Total Place is about expecting citizens to do more for themselves	−2	−2	−1	0
42	Total Place is about understanding people who are non-users of services	1	−1	−1	−1

Table 9.3 Total Place respondents and factor loadings

		1	2	3	4
BS1	Senior LA	0.37	0.4017	0.1025	0.4493
SM2	Middle Statutory	0.0184	0.4345	0.5176	0.3936
SM3	Middle Statutory	0.4748	0.4924	0.1915	0.2574
BM4	Middle LA	0.252	0.5924X	0.2885	−0.0096
BS5	Senior LA	−0.2318	0.4639	0.246	0.448
BS6	Senior LA	−0.0155	0.1943	0.0513	0.4458X
VS7	Senior Voluntary	0.0068	−0.1225	−0.3247	0.6187X
VS8	Senior Voluntary	−0.0256	0.1574	0.7118X	0.3694
BM9	Middle LA	0.4809X	0.1402	−0.0802	−0.0095
VS10	Senior Voluntary	0.2226	0.4074	0.3348	0.5483
VS11	Senior Voluntary	0.1758	−0.232	0.2554	0.2766
BM12	Middle LA	0.2347	0.3672	0.2483	0.3559
VF13	Frontline Voluntary	0.3611	0.1383	0.2676	0.374
VS14	Senior Voluntary	0.3291	0.2218	0.2843	0.4647
VM15	Middle Voluntary	0.3227	0.3278	0.1856	0.429
BM16	Middle LA	0.2808	0.4536	0.3233	0.2464
SM17	Middle Statutory	0.4821	−0.0909	0.5990X	0.1286
SM18	Middle Statutory	0.6684X	0.0835	0.3204	0.0021
BM19	Middle LA	0.5256X	0.0698	−0.0548	0.1857
BM20	Middle LA	0.6478X	0.2133	0.1803	0.1557
OS21	Senior 'Other'	0.1063	0.5846X	−0.0698	0.2745
BF22	Frontline LA	0.6804X	−0.0291	0.2855	0.0424
SS23	Senior Statutory	0.4979	0.1932	0.1866	0.4948
BM24	Middle LA	0.6347X	0.2464	0.0403	0.4026
BM25	Middle LA	0.5022X	0.0084	0.2131	0.2146
BM26	Middle LA	0.399	0.4144	0.5722	0.2596
OM27	Middle 'Other'	0.5643	0.54	0.3094	0.2227
BF28	Frontline LA	0.4822X	0.3528	−0.0888	−0.0332
BM29	Middle LA	0.3354	0.3721	0.3775	0.3988
BF30	Frontline LA	0.2758	0.048	0.0055	0.4606X
BM31	Middle LA	0.0948	0.316	0.5185X	0.3637
CC32	Community Sector	0.5462X	−0.2819	0.27	0.1697
BM33	Middle LA	0.3246	0.5659X	0.4311	−0.0128
VM34	Middle Voluntary	0.4814	0.2316	0.4589	0.381
BF35	Frontline LA	0.5526X	0.2826	0.2018	0.3256
OF36	Frontline 'Other'	0.2397	0.5410X	0.2309	0.4095
BM37	Middle LA	0.0838	0.0679	0.276	0.6198X
SS38	Senior Statutory	0.3134	0.3731	0.5478X	−0.0898
BM39	Middle LA	0.1981	0.6518X	0.0815	0.1506
BM40	Middle LA	−0.0216	0.1966	0.7230X	−0.0219
VF41	Frontline Voluntary	0.7889X	0.0544	0.4239	−0.0478
BS42	Senior LA	0.4162X	0.0335	0.1948	0.2699
SS43	Senior Statutory	0.6102X	0.2212	0.4243	0.0611
SM44	Middle Statutory	0.1784	0.4826X	0.0763	0.2665

Table 9.3   (Continued)

		1	2	3	4
BM45	Middle LA	−0.3079	0.6058X	0.1002	0.2463
OS46	Senior 'Other'	0.1063	0.2128	0.5795X	0.0983
BS47	Senior LA	−0.3663	0.1741	−0.376	0.4866
BF48	Frontline LA	0.5699X	0.1877	0.0581	−0.1234
VS49	Senior Voluntary	0.3269	0.2772	0.5034X	0.2521
BS50	Senior LA	0.2875	−0.2034	0.5981X	0.3202
BF51	Frontline LA	0.3666	0.1928	0.0749	0.3221
BM52	Middle LA	0.3121	0.0672	0.6325X	0.0355
BS53	Senior LA	0.5525X	0.1525	0.3078	0.1541
VS54	Senior Voluntary	0.3913	0.4328	0.329	−0.0471
BM55	Middle LA	−0.3198	0.6285X	0.2364	0.3282
SM56	Middle Statutory	0.4823	0.3729	0.4507	0.2027
SM57	Middle Statutory	0.1118	0.5656X	0.5524	0.0217
VS58	Senior Voluntary	−0.0455	0.2839	0.3386	0.6747X
BM59	Middle LA	0.1987	0.117	0.6258X	0.3085
VM60	Middle Voluntary	0.1576	0.7114X	0.1771	0.108
OS61	Senior 'Other'	0.1063	0.5675X	0.272	−0.0463
BS62	Senior LA	0.332	0.2768	0.2581	0.3636
BS63	Senior LA	0.1275	0.3666	0.3175	0.4625
BM64	Middle LA	0.1743	0.5726X	−0.1509	0.1059

Chapter 4 Q methodology study of Total Place

Q methodology analysis process

Q researchers mostly use one of two dedicated Q analysis software packages to correlate and factorise their Q sort data. The object of the analysis is to compare the sorting grid of each respondent, pair-wise, in order to generate a correlation matrix. By comparing how Person A sorted Statement 1 with how Person B sorted Statement 1, and repeating this for Statements 2, 3, 4 and so on, it is possible to quantify the difference between Person A and Person B. This is possible because a standard set of statements, instructions and sorting grid were used. Q methodologists use centroid factor analysis to *extract* potential factors from the correlation matrix. If Person A, Person C, Person G and Person M are all correlated, the first round of extraction will remove their commonality from the matrix. This is Factor 1. With their community removed the relationships in the matrix are modified. A second cluster is identified and removed. This is repeated until no further clusters can be found.

Choosing a factor solution

Following the process of factor extraction from the correlation matrix, Q analysis seeks to produce idealised Q sorts based on the loading of respondents whose sorts most closely inform the factors extracted. No one respondent's sort will quite match the idealised sort based on the extracted factors, but those whose own sorts are closely correlated with the extracted factor are manually flagged by the researcher and will then inform the production of synthetic factor arrays, proportionate to their proximity with the factor. A four-factor solution produces four-factor arrays that are then ripe for further analysis and interpretation.

The use of software to conduct the extraction of factors removes the need for laborious pair-wise calculations, but there remains a need for the researcher to exercise judgement throughout the process. The most important decision required of the researcher in a Q study is to choose how many factors to interpret. The researcher will usually explore a range of solutions: ranging from one to seven factors. Although there are a multitude of approaches and tests that can be applied to help in this decision-making (see Watts & Stenner, 2012), a factor solution is rejected if the weakest factor does not reflect a shared point of view, that is, when the weakest factor in a possible solution has only one person-loading. There are instances when a single person factor might be retained, but these are usually where that single person is either the researcher themselves or of distinct or theoretical interest to the study (the boss among employees, a doctor among nurses, a professor among students).

A further consideration for the researcher when choosing the factor solution is when the weakest factor is insufficiently distinct. Unless the topic under study is something as divisive as abortion or animal rights, all the factors will be to some extent similar, but should be significantly distinct. When justifying their four-factor solution, Dryzek and Berejikian stated succinctly, 'the extraction of additional factors produced, upon interpretation, a lack of clear distinction across two or more of the factors' (Dryzek & Berejikian, 1993, p. 5).

Interpreting Q factors

The output of a software analysis programme such as PQmethod comes in the form of a 'list file', known commonly by its filename extension '.lis'. This is usually 40 or 50 pages of tables that often baffles and intimidates the first-time Q researcher. With experience, Q methodologists come to realise the lis file is a summary of two or three outputs reported in several ways.

It is the lis file document that offers the starting point for interpreting the factors. Q interpretation usually starts with Factor 1 and the factor arrays. Q researchers often use the factor array to physically sort the statements into the shape of the response grid. Researchers start by focusing on the extremes of the grid: what were the statements people on this factor feel most strongly about? Usually a pattern starts to form; it is advisable to start capturing these patterns, perhaps trying to name or characterise the factor based on these statements at the edges of the grid. However it is also important not to overlook the centrally placed statements. Their relative indifference to a statement can also be revealing. Furthermore, you have to acknowledge the possibility they agreed with more of the statements than those with which they disagreed, and therefore zero does not automatically mean neutral or –1 mean disagreement. For all of these reasons the factor array has to be considered holistically if we are to begin to understand the character of the idealised factor.

Having drawn out the character from the factor array, it is then possible to explore what is distinctive about the placing of the statements. For example, are there statements placed highly in Factor 1 that all other factors place neutrally or negatively? Which of the statements make that factor, in a sense, unique? Finally the researcher turns to finding out who informed the factor, and which of the Q sorts loaded highly on the factor. The three or four respondents with the highest loading are known as the factor exemplars. Their Q sorts exemplify the shared viewpoint. If additional data has been collected on these exemplars, such as interview transcripts or written accounts, these become invaluable and can be used to inform the emerging characterisation of the factor.

It should be noted that not every respondent will load cleanly on a factor. Some people are mavericks, others give erroneous or rushed responses. The presence of people in the study not loading on a factor is not a failure of the study, it is a finding. That said, most Q studies overlook the mavericks, the confounded and the non-significant, and instead direct their attention to the shared viewpoints.

It is also worth mentioning a particular category of statements in a Q study known as consensus statements. Consensus statements are those that do not distinguish between any pair of factors, in other words most of the factors place them in generally the same way. In some studies a statement can be placed positively by all factors. In a previous study all factors agreed with a particular statement, it seems because it focused on the importance of trust when working in a partnership (Jeffares & Skelcher, 2011). However, on further examination the reason for agreement with this statement differed across the factors. In that sense consensus is revealing. Another type of consensus is where all factors place a statement indifferently. Ideally if these are identified during piloting, the indifference can suggest revision or removal of the statement. This type of consensus prompts reflection among the researchers to think why they included the statement in the first place and whether the consensus was in part down to how it was phrased, or about the choice of theme, or both.

Chapter 6 social media study

APIs, garden hoses and fire hoses

The API or Application Programming Interface is the access portal through which social media platforms allow people to capture their data. Users who sign up to the sites usually do so for free, and agree to the terms and conditions that usually allow the website owner to sell their data and export it to third party companies, along with subjecting users to advertisements.

Along with this discussion of APIs it is also worth noting that there are at least two main types of feed – one is rate limited, offering a sample, the second is the full feed, offering complete transactional data. The precise percentage of what is captured is not always clear. Some claim the public API can be just 1% of the total flow.

API vs firehose

A comparison of API verses firehose (gnip.com's PowerTrack feed) collecting tweets on Margaret Thatcher's funeral showed that over a 24 hour period, the API captured 57.5% of total tweets. There were times where the rate hit 30,000 per hour. During this time, the percentage captured dropped to just 30%. In contrast, once the rates dropped to around 1,000 an hour, the API captured close to 98% of tweets. Therefore, how much of a problem this is depends on the volume and velocity of the topic studied and whether the claims the research is seeking to make require transactional data rather than a sample.

Sentiment meters – example of Topsy.com

Topsy explain how their sentiment meter works with the following statement:

Topsy social sentiment is computed for millions of terms, based on hundreds of millions of tweets every day. It is tailored to the informal and abbreviated language that is often found in tweets and social media in general, and normalized for each term based on scores for all other terms used in Twitter. Topsy's social sentiment uses a proprietary in-house curated dictionary of sentiment weighted words and phrases to fine-tune its sentiment algorithm to handle Twitter's unique 140 character limits and 'twitterisms'. By combining some English grammar rules to this, Topsy is able to accurately fine-tune results in relatively high accuracy rates, with results typically garnering a 70% agreement rate with manually reviewed content. Aiding this is the ability to identify and ignore entities with misleading names (e.g. Angry Birds) and applying stemming and lemmatization to expand the sentiment dictionary scope. Currently, Topsy social sentiment only works for the English language.

> (*Source*: Topsy.com 2013 http://help.topsy.com/customer/portal/
> articles/669162-sentiment-analysis-methodology)

The sentiment measurement of PCC and MyPCC

Topsy suggest, using firehose data, that during the collection period there was 88,165 tweets about #PCC or #MyPCC made – with 14,036 negative and 17,140 positive. This breaks down as 82,613, 14,036 & 15,545 for #PCC and 5,552; 680 and 1,595 for #MyPCC respectively.

Clustering thresholds

When using DiscoverText to cluster Twitter data, it seems choice threshold matters little between 65% and 85%. For example, in an illustrative set of 213 (from an example project called Transforming Rehabilitation), de-duplication reduced the set to 129. When applying a 60% threshold it identifies that within this set there are 40 clusters of two and the rest are single items. Only when raised above 85% did it reduce the number of found clusters to 37. At a 95% threshold, the machine classifier cannot distinguish the near-duplicates and suggests only one cluster. Retaining the clustering at 60% allowed for the creation of a new dataset of just 84 formed of the single items and one item from each cluster – also known as cluster seeds.

H-indexes

In contrast with the PCC H-Index score of 24, the Transforming Rehabilitation dataset had an H of two, and only two had more than two. An alternative metric in citations is the I-10 index, which is simply the number of publications with at least ten citations. In publishing, this H-index is a measure of esteem for the author. Comparing H-index by issue in this way compares the degree to which the issue has gravitated

Table 9.4 Ten policy ideas compared by cluster size

Policy idea	Clusters	H	I10	C1	C % of N DD
10p Tax	4668	55	139	188	0.43%
Bedroom Tax	908	11	12	27	0.54%
Bristol Mayor	1883	6	1	14	0.16%
Hospital Food	196	9	9	112	5.67%
HS2	3023	16	27	116	0.44%
Mansion Tax	600	10	11	62	1.85%
Thatcherism	592	12	14	365	8.54%
Minimum Price	1244	12	15	73	0.81%
Big Society	346	4	1	12	0.62%
Work Programme	1083	11	13	131	2.50%

around a limited set of story-lines. For example, Table 9.4 shows the comparison of ten policy ideas and the clusters generated. The archives varied in size, but the H-indexes are broadly comparable, where around ten clusters of ten or more are to be found. Also explored here is the size of the largest cluster as a percentage of the de-duplicated items. Both Thatcherism and Hospital Food archives contained a large cluster that dominated in the archive. The purpose of clustering in this case is to identify if any particular tweet is dominating.

Filtering by Klout score

Filtering by Klout scores of 65+ drastically reduces the size of the dataset. For example, from an archive of 6,372 tweets discussing whether Margaret Thatcher was entitled to a state funeral, only 59 tweets were made by users with Klout of 65+.

Chapter 7 social media study

Thematic coding of PCC – advice to coders

Additional information given to coders to improve thematic coding

Information This could be improved by adding all items that discuss information into the category. When discussing information, the items often attribute praise or blame to specific actors (e.g. organisers, local government or Home Office, government, candidates) – and sometimes they do not. All items discussing information should be coded as 'Information'.

Politicisation This code is for any argument that this is leading to politicisation of policing.

Exceptions: In the earlier codeset, we suggested that any mention of politicisation in order to support a vote for independents was not a valid statement. However it is not always clear whether the link is made with independents – so on balance ALL explicit mention of politicising the police should be coded.

Candidates This should only code opinion regarding the skills, aptitude, suitability or performance of candidates.

Exceptions: However if regarding candidate performance in giving information, this should be coded 'Information'. If discussing specific candidates/parties, this should be coded as 'Not Statement'.

Organisers This code focuses on the performance of those thought to be organising the election, known or unknown. It could include mention of government, Cameron, Home Office, Tories or local government, 'The man'. These items discuss the quality of the election or its implementation of the policy.

A common use of #hashtags such as #farce or #shambles suggests poor organisation.

Exceptions: Any discussion of organisation regarding information should be coded 'Information'.

Any discussion of the importance of the policy should be coded 'Other'.

Vote This should be used to code items that either advocate voting or not voting. This might also include those who express this as a personal or moral dilemma.

Exceptions: If reason not to vote is based on information.

Cost (new code) This should include any discussion regarding the cost, expense, waste of money or value for money.

Other (0.54) Makes up 25% of the set. So one in four times it is in Other – what is in here? This is a mixed bag. Includes a general statement that this is a bad idea or good idea, 'not public role to choose', electoral system, discussion of turnout, mandate, democracy, spoiling ballots, privatisation of policing or managerialisation.

Exceptions: Where it discusses other codes such as cost, info, candidate performance, organisers or candidates.

Not statements We should not be timid about suggesting something is not a statement. If we were 80% accurate in the first round of coding then it is to be expected that 20% are not statements in this dataset. We should not feel obliged to code them. They should be dispatched. Any critique of parties or specific candidates.

Not sure – if you are not sure, do not feel forced to make a choice just because you have 8 codes available. Click 'not sure'.

Thematic coding of PCC data coded 'Other'

To explore the emergence of additional themes, we created a dataset of tweets solely from the 16th November, the day that the results were announced. It is suggested that tweets with the hashtag PCC came to 40,114 that day; contrast this with 28,000 the previous day and 28,000 in the previous 18 days. This was by far the peak day of activity around the PCC hashtag. To put it into perspective, the following 12 days had just 9,000 #PCC tweets. Using the API 68.9% of the 40,114 tweets were collected. The fetch also pulled in PCC, fetch duplicates were disallowed and a total set of 47,159 was collected.

On the PCC16N we ran the Statement/Not statement classifier, based on the coding of 14,000 items. We split the dataset at a certainty threshold of 0.85, giving a new dataset of 50% opinionated tweets.

Compassionate care, comparison of sources

The following sources were included in the study:

- The *Daily Mail* article – http://www.dailymail.co.uk/debate/article-2313232/Royal-College-Nursing-union-puts-patient-care-last.html#comments (52 comments)
- *The Daily Telegraph* – http://www.telegraph.co.uk/health/healthnews/10009491/Hunts-nurse-training-plan-is-really-stupid-says-union-leader.html#disqus_thread (80 comments).
- *The Independent* – http://www.independent.co.uk/life-style/health-and-families/health-news/david-cameron-hits-back-after-nursing-leaders-raise-major-concerns-over-staffing-levels-and-governments-

plan-to-get-trainee-nurses-working-as-healthcare-assistants-8582081
.html?origin=internalSearch#disqus_thread (146 Comments)

- *The Guardian* – http://www.guardian.co.uk/society/2013/apr/22/
cameron-hunt-rcn-nurse-training#show-all (750 comments)
- *Nursing Times* – Facebook discussion, 26th March http://www
.facebook.com/EMAP.NT?fref=ts (213 posts).
- *Nursing Standard*, Facebook Discussion, 24th March 2013 (120
Comments).
- Royal College of Nursing Facebook page – http://www.facebook.com/
royalcollegeofnursing (131 posts).
- Twitter (974 tweets) collected using API searching for 'nurse training'
and 'compassionate care'.

References

Aharony, N. (2012). Twitter use by three political leaders: An exploratory analysis. *Online Information Review*, 36(4), 587–603. doi: 10.1108/14684521211254086

Alcock, Pete. (2010). Building the Big Society: A new policy environment for the third sector in England. *Voluntary Sector Review*, 1(3), 379–389.

Alexa. (2013). *Twitter.com Site Info*. Retrieved from http://www.alexa.com/siteinfo/twitter.com, accessed 26 June 2013.

Algeo, J. (1993). *Fifty Years among the New Words: A Dictionary of Neologisms 1941–1991*. Cambridge: Cambridge University Press.

Allen, Richard. (1995). On a clear day you can have a vision: A visioning model for everyone. *Leadership & Organization Development Journal*, 16(4), 39–44.

Allmendinger, P. (2005). Applying Lacanian insight and a dash of Derridean deconstruction to planning's 'Dark Side'. *Planning Theory*, 4(1), 87–112. doi: 10.1177/1473095205051444

Ampofo, L., Anstead, N. & O'Loughlin, B. (2011). Trust, confidence, and credibility: Citizen responses on Twitter to opinion polls during the 2010 UK general election. *Information Communication & Society*, 14(6), 850–871. doi: 10.1080/1369118x.2011.587882

Angus, Daniel, Rintel, Sean & Wiles, Janet. (2013). Making sense of big text: A visual-first approach for analysing text data using Leximancer and Discursis. *International Journal of Social Research Methodology*, 16(3), 261–267.

Anstead, N. & O'Loughlin, B. (2011). The emerging viewertariat and BBC question time: Television debate and real-time commenting online. *International Journal of Press-Politics*, 16(4), 440–462. doi: 10.1177/1940161211415519

Arceneaux, N. & Weiss, A. S. (2010). Seems stupid until you try it: Press coverage of Twitter, 2006–2009. *New Media & Society*, 12(8), 1262–1279. doi: 10.1177/1461444809360773

Armstrong, C. L. & Gao, F. F. (2011). Gender, Twitter and news content an examination across platforms and coverage areas. *Journalism Studies*, 12(4), 490–505. doi: 10.1080/1461670x.2010.527548

Asur, Sitaram & Huberman, Bernardo A. (2010). *Predicting the Future with Social Media*. Paper presented at the International Conference on Web Intelligence and Intelligent Agent Technology (WI-IAT), 2010 IEEE/WIC/ACM.

Auer, M. R. (2011). The policy sciences of social media. *Policy Studies Journal*, 39(4), 709–736. doi: 10.1111/j.1541-0072.2011.00428.x

Bagasheva, Alexandra (2011). Compound verbs in English revisited. *Bucharest Working Papers in Linguistics*, 1, 125–151.

Bailey, N. & Pill, M. (2011). The continuing popularity of the neighbourhood and neighbourhood governance in the transition from the 'big state' to the 'big society' paradigm. *Environment and Planning C: Government and Policy*, 29(5), 927–942.

Baker, Keith. (2008). *Strategic Service Partnerships ad Boundary-Spanning Behaviour' A Study of Muliple Cascading Policy Windows*. Unpublished PhD thesis: University of Birmingham.

Baker, Rachel. (2006). Economic rationality and health and lifestyle choices for people with diabetes. *Social Science & Medicine*, 63(9), 2341–2353.

Baker, Rachel, Thompson, Carl & Mannion, Russel. (2006). Q methodology in health economics. *Journal of Health Services Research & Policy*, 11(1), 38–45.

Bardach, Eugene. (1976). Policy termination as a political process. *Policy Sciences*, 7(2), 123–131.

Barwise, P. & Meehan, S. (2010). The one thing you must get right when building a brand. *Harvard Business Review*, 88(12), 80–84.

Baxter, G., Marcella, R. & Varfis, E. (2011). The use of the internet by political parties and candidates in Scotland during the 2010 UK general election campaign. *Aslib Proceedings*, 63(5), 464–483. doi: 10.1108/00012531111164969

BCSP. (2002). *Towards a Community Strategy for Birmingham 2002–2003*. Birmingham: Birmingham City Strategic Partnership.

BDO. (2013). From Housing and Litter to Facebook and Twitter: Updating Your Status. http://static.bdo.uk.com/assets/documents/2012/03/BDO_Local_Government_Team_Updating_your_status_social_media_report.pdf, accessed 22 June 2013.

Behn, Robert, D. (1978). How to terminate a public policy: A dozen hints for the would-be terminator. *Policy Analysis*, 4(3), 393–413.

Benczes, Réka. (2006). *Creative Compounding in English: The Semantics of Metaphorical and Metonymical Noun-noun Combinations* (Vol. 19). Philadelphia, PA: John Benjamins Publishing.

Bennett, T., Grossberg, L. & Morris, M. (2005). *New Keywords: A Revised Vocabulary of Culture and Society*. London: Wiley-Blackwell.

Berman, S. (2009). *The Social Democratic Moment: Ideas and Politics in the Making of Interwar Europe*. Harvard University Press.

Beyer, Yngvil. (2012). Using DiscoverText for Large Scale Twitter Harvesting, in Microform & Digitization Review Vol 41, Issue 3–4, pp 121–125.

Binder, A. R. (2012). Figuring out #Fukushima: An initial look at functions and content of US Twitter commentary about nuclear risk. *Environmental Communication-a Journal of Nature and Culture*, 6(2), 268–277. doi: 10.1080/17524032.2012.672442

Bjørkelund, Eivind, Burnett, Thomas H. & Nørvåg, Kjetil. (2012). A study of opinion mining and visualization of hotel reviews. *Proceedings of the 14th International Conference on Information Integration and Web-based Applications & Services*: ACM.

Blyth, Mark. (1997). "Any More Bright Ideas?" The ideational turn of comparative political economy. *Comparative Politics*, 29 (2), 229–250.

Blyth, Mark. (2002). *Great Transformations: Economic Ideas and Institutional Change in the Twentieth Century*. Cambridge: Cambridge University Press.

Blyth, Mark. (2013). *Austerity: The History of a Dangerous Idea*. OUP USA.

Boin, Arjen, Kuipers, Sanneke & Steenbergen, Marco. (2010). The life and death of public organizations: A question of institutional design? *Governance*, 23(3), 385–410.

Bollen, Johan, Mao, Huina & Zeng, Xiaojun. (2011). Twitter mood predicts the stock market. *Journal of Computational Science*, 2(1), 1–8.

Bosch, T. (2012). Blogging and tweeting climate change in South Africa. *Ecquid Novi-African Journalism Studies*, 33(1), 44–53. doi: 10.1080/02560054.2011.636825

Bovens, Mark. (1998). *The Quest for Responsibility: Accountability and Citizenship in Complex Organisations*. Cambridge: Cambridge University Press.

Bowen, Glenn A. (2008). Naturalistic inquiry and the saturation concept: A research note. *Qualitative Research*, 8(1), 137–152.

Boyd, D. & Crawford, K. (2012). Critical questions for big data provocations for a cultural, technological, and scholarly phenomenon. *Information Communication & Society*, 15(5), 662–679. doi: 10.1080/1369118x.2012.678878

Bratich, J. (2011). User-Generated discontent: Convergence, polemology and dissent. *Cultural Studies*, 25(4–5), 621–640. doi: 10.1080/09502386.2011.600552

Braun, Dietmar & Busch, Andreas (eds.) (1999). *Public Policy and Political Ideas*. Cheltenham: Edward Elgar.

Brewer, Gene A., Selden, Sally Coleman, Facer, I. I. & Rex, L. (2000). Individual conceptions of public service motivation. *Public Administration Review*, 60(3), 254–264.

Brindle, David. (2009). 'Billions could be saved' in Public Services Revamp, Total Place Finds, *The Guardian*. Retrieved from http://www.guardian.co.uk/politics/2009/sep/29/thinktanks-policy

Briones, R. L., Kuch, B., Liu, B. F. & Jin, Y. (2011). Keeping up with the digital age: How the American red cross uses social media to build relationships. *Public Relations Review*, 37(1), 37–43. doi: 10.1016/j.pubrev.2010.12.006

Brown, Steven R. (1980). *Political Subjectivity: Applications of Q Methodology in Political Science*. Cambridge: Yale University Press.

Brown, Steven R. (1986). Q technique and method: Principles and procedures. In Berry, W. D. and Lewis-Beck, M. S. (eds.) *New Tools for Social Scientists: Advances and Applications in Research Methods*, London: Sage, 57–76.

Brown, Steven R. (1993). A primer on Q methodology. *Operant Subjectivity*, 16(3/4), 91–138.

Bruns, A. (2012). Journalists and Twitter: How Australian news organisations adapt to a new medium. *Media International Australia*, Number 144, 97–107.

Callahan, Kathe, Dubnick, Melvin J. & Olshfski, Dorothy. (2006). War narratives: Framing our understanding of the war on terror. *Public Administration Review*, 66(4), 554–568.

Cameron, David. (2009). The Big Society. *Hugo Young Lecture*, 10 November 09.

Campbell, John L. (2002). Ideas, politics, and public policy. *Annual Review of Sociology*, 28, 21–38.

Carlbom, Aje. (2006). An empty signifier: The blue-and-yellow Islam of Sweden. *Journal of Muslim Minority Affairs*, 26(2), 245–261.

Carpenter, C. & Drezner, D. W. (2010). International relations 2.0: The implications of new media for an old profession. *International Studies Perspectives*, 11(3), 255–272. doi: 10.1111/j.1528-3585.2010.00407.x

Carr, S. (2011). How we long to believe that our wise leaders know what's going on. *Independent*. (15 February 2011).

Cha, M., Benevenuto, F., Haddadi, H. & Gummadi, K. (2012). The world of connections and information flow in Twitter. *IEEE Transactions on Systems Man and Cybernetics Part a-Systems and Humans*, 42(4), 991–998. doi: 10.1109/tsmca.2012.2183359

Chadwick, A. (2011). The political information cycle in a hybrid news system: The British prime minister and the 'Bullygate' affair. *International Journal of Press-Politics*, 16(1), 3–29. doi: 10.1177/1940161210384730

Chen, G. M. (2011). Tweet this: A uses and gratifications perspective on how active Twitter use gratifies a need to connect with others. *Computers in Human Behavior*, 27(2), 755–762. doi: 10.1016/j.chb.2010.10.023

Cheng, J. S., Sun, A., Hu, D. N. & Zeng, D. (2011). An information diffusion-based recommendation framework for micro-blogging. *Journal of the Association for Information Systems*, 12(7), 463–486.

Chesterman, A. (1997). *Memes of Translation: The Spread of Ideas in Translation Theory*. Philadelphia, PA: John Benjamins Publishing Company.

Chi, F. & Yang, N. (2011). Twitter Adoption in Congress. *Review of Network Economics*, 10(1), 45. doi: 10.2202/1446-9022.1255

Cho, S. E. & Park, H. W. (2012). Government organizations' innovative use of the internet: The case of the Twitter activity of South Korea's Ministry for Food, Agriculture, Forestry and Fisheries. *Scientometrics*, 90(1), 9–23. doi: 10.1007/s11192-011-0519-2

Choi, Hyunyoung & Varian, Hal. (2012). Predicting the present with Google Trends. *Economic Record*, 88(s1), 2–9.

Christenson, Dale & Walker, Derek H. T. (2008). Using vision as a critical success element in project management. *International Journal of Managing Projects in Business*, 1(4), 611–622.

Cohen, Michael D., March, James G. & Olsen, Johan P. (1972). A garbage can model of organizational choice. *Administrative Science Quarterly*, 1–25.

Coke, James G. & Brown, Steven R. (1976). Public attitudes about land use policy and their impact on state policy-makers. *Publius: The Journal of Federalism*, 6(1), 97–134.

Connor, Neil. (2002). Better together: Charter marks up a century, *Birmingham Post*, 29 July 2002, 3.

Cornford, James. (1990). Performing fleas: Reflections from a think tank. *Policy Studies*, 11(4), 22–30.

Cornwall, Andrea. (2007). Buzzwords and fuzzwords: Deconstructing development discourse. *Development in Practice*, 17(4–5), 471–484. doi: 10.1080/09614520701469302

Cornwall, Andrea & Eade, Deborah. (2010). *Deconstructing Development Discourse: Buzzwords and Fuzzwords*. Rugby: Practical Action Publishing.

Cotterill, Sarah, Moseley, Alice & Richardson, Liz. (2012). Can nudging create the Big Society? Experiments in civic behaviour and implications for the voluntary and public sectors. *Voluntary Sector Review*, 3(2), 265–274.

Crawford, K. (2009). Following you: Disciplines of listening in social media. *Continuum-Journal of Media & Cultural Studies*, 23(4), 525–535. doi: 10.1080/10304310903003270

Crowdverb. (2012). *Crowdverb*. Retrieved from http://crowdverb.com/what-we-do/products/csa/issue.

Culnan, M. J., McHugh, P. J. & Zubillaga, J. I. (2010). How large U.S. companies can use Twitter and other social media to gain business value. *Mis Quarterly Executive*, 9(4), 243–259.

Cuppen, Eefje. (2010). Putting perspectives into participation: Constructive conflict methodology for problem structuring in stakeholder dialogues (Oisterwijk: Uitgeverij BOXPress).

Cuppen, Eefje, Breukers, Sylvia, Hisschemöller, Matthijs & Bergsma, Emmy. (2010). Q methodology to select participants for a stakeholder dialogue on energy options from biomass in the Netherlands. *Ecological Economics*, 69(3), 579–591.

Dale, P. (2001). Council set to get power to the people. *Birmingham Post*, 22 September 2001, 6.

Dale, Paul. (2012). A little less conversation please, blog post on *The Chamberlain Files*. Retrieved from http://www.thechamberlainfiles.com/a-little -less-conversation-please/5362 *The Chamberlain Files*.

Davies, J. S. & Pill, M. (2012). Empowerment or abandonment? Prospects for neighbourhood revitalization under the Big Society. *Public Money Management*, 32(3), 193–200.

Day, Shane. (2008). Applications of Q methodology to a variety of policy process theories and frameworks. *International Journal of Organization Theory and Behavior*, 11(2), 141.

de Graaf, G. (2010). The loyalties of top public administrators. *Journal of Public Administration Research and Theory*, 21(2), 285–306. doi: 10.1093/jopart/ muq028

de Graaf, Gjalt & Van Exel, Job. (2008). Using Q methodology in administrative ethics. *Public Integrity*, 11(1), 63–78.

DeLeon, Peter. (1977). Public policy termination: An end and a beginning. Santa Monica, CA: RAND Corporation.

Department of Work & Pensions. (2012). *Social Media Case Study – Convergence Partnership in Cornwall and the Isles of Scilly – ESF*. Retrieved from http://www.dwp.gov.uk/esf/resources/publicity/social-media/convergence -cornwall.

Dickinson, Helen, Jeffares, Stephen, Nicholds, Alyson & Glasby, Jon. (2013). Beyond the Berlin wall? Investigating joint commissioning and its various meanings using a Q methodology approach. *Public Management Review*(ahead-of-print), 1–22. **doi:**10.1080/14719037.2012.757353

DiscoverText. (2013). *DiscoverText*. Retrieved from http://www.discovertext.com, accessed 22 June 2013.

Docherty, C. (2002). Council to lift lid on plans for housing. *Birmingham Post*, 19 August 2002.

Downs, Anthony. (1972). Up and down with ecology: The issue attention cycle. *Public Interest*, 28(1), 38–50.

Dryzek, John S. & Berejikian, Jeffrey. (1993). Reconstructing democratic theory. *American Political Science Review*, 87(1), 48–60.

Dudley, G. & Richardson, J. (2001). *Why Does Policy Change?: Lessons from British Transport Policy 1945–99*. Abingdon: Taylor & Francis.

Durning, D. (1999). The transition from traditional to postpositivist policy analysis: A role for Q-methodology. *Journal of Policy Analysis and Management*, 18(3), 389–410.

Ebner, M., Lienhardt, C., Rohs, M. & Meyer, I. (2010). Microblogs in higher education – a chance to facilitate informal and process-oriented learning? *Computers & Education*, 55(1), 92–100. doi: 10.1016/j.compedu.2009.12.006

Edelman, M. J. (1977). *Political Language: Words that Succeed and Policies that Fail*. New York: Academic Press.

Efron, M. (2011). Information search and retrieval in microblogs. *Journal of the American Society for Information Science and Technology*, 62(6), 996–1008. doi: 10.1002/asi.21512

Electoral Commission. (2013). Policy and Crime Commissioner elections in England and Wales: Report on the administration of the elections held on 15 November 2012, Electoral Commission

Ellis, G., Barry, J. & Robinson, C. (2007). Many ways to say 'no', different ways to say 'yes': Applying Q-methodology to understand public acceptance of wind farm proposals. *Journal of Environmental Planning and Management*, 50(4), 517–551. doi: 10.1080/09640560701402075

Eshuis, Jasper & Edwards, Arthur. (2012). Branding the city: The democratic legitimacy of a new mode of governance. *Urban Studies*, 50(5), 1066–1082.

Evans, Kathy. (2011). 'Big Society'in the UK: A policy review. *Children & Society*, 25(2), 164–171.

Fenn, Jackie & LeHong, Hung. (2011). Hype cycle for emerging technologies. Stamford, CT: *Gartner*, July.

Ferry, Martin & Bachtler, John. (2013). Reassessing the concept of policy termination: The case of regional policy in England. *Policy Studies*, 34(3), 255–273.

Finlayson, Alan. (2004). Political science, political ideas and rhetoric. *Economy and Society*, 33(4), 528–549.

Fisher, R. A. (1971). *The Design of Experiments*. Hafner Publishing Company.

Fotaki, Marianna. (2010). Why do public policies fail so often? Exploring health policy-making as an imaginary and symbolic construction. *Organization*, 17(6), 703–720, 1350–5084.

Francis, R. (2013). *Report of the Mid Staffordshire NHS Foundation Trust Public Inquiry*. London: Stationery Office. Retrieved from http://www.midstaffspublicinquiry.com/report.

Frazer, J. G. (2009). *The Golden Bough: A Study of Magic and Religion*. Floating Press.

Friedman, S. M. (2011). Three mile Island, Chernobyl, and Fukushima: An analysis of traditional and new media coverage of nuclear accidents and radiation. *Bulletin of the Atomic Scientists*, 67(5), 55–65. doi: 10.1177/0096340211421587

Froud, J., Haslam, C., Johal, S., Shaoul, J. & Williams, K. (1998). Persuasion without numbers?: Public policy and the justification of capital charging in NHS trust hospitals. *Accounting, Auditing & Accountability Journal*, 11(1), 99–125.

Gimson, A. (2011). Those who came to scoff leave with an empty stomach, *Daily Telegraph*, 15 February 2011.

Gladwell, M. (2006). *The Tipping Point: How Little Things Can Make a Big Difference*. New York: Little Brown.

Glasman, M. & Norman, J. (2012). The Big Society in question. *Political Quarterly*, 82, 9–21.

Glasze, Georg. (2007). The discursive constitution of a world-spanning region and the role of empty signifiers: The case of Francophonia. *Geopolitics*, 12(4), 656–679.

Glynos, Jason & Howarth, David Robert. (2007). *Logics of Critical Explanation in Social and Political Theory*. London: Routledge.

Gofas, Andreas. (2009). Ideas and Interests in the Construction of EMU: Beyond the Rationalist Bias of the New Ideational Orthodoxy, CSGR Working Paper No. 76/01. Retrieved from http://dspace.cigilibrary.org/jspui/handle/123456789/9134

Gofas, Andreas & Hay, Colin. (2012). *The Role of Ideas in Political Analysis: A Portrait of Contemporary Debates*. Abingdon: Taylor & Francis Group.

Golbeck, J., Grimes, J. M. & Rogers, A. (2010). Twitter use by the US congress. *Journal of the American Society for Information Science and Technology*, 61(8), 1612–1621. doi: 10.1002/asi.21344

Goldstein, J. & Keohane, R. O. (1993). *Ideas and Foreign Policy: Beliefs, Institutions, and Political Change*. Ithaca, NY: Cornell University Press.

Goncalves, B., Perra, N. & Vespignani, A. (2011). Modeling users' activity on Twitter networks: Validation of Dunbar's number. *Plos One*, 6(8), 5. doi: 10.1371/journal.pone.0022656

Gonzalez-Bailon, S., Borge-Holthoefer, J., Rivero, A. & Moreno, Y. (2011). The dynamics of protest recruitment through an online network. *Scientific Reports*, 1, 7. doi: 10.1038/srep00197

González-Gaudiano, Edgar. (2005). Education for sustainable development: configuration and meaning. *Policy Futures in Education*, 3(3), 243–250.

Grant, W. J., Moon, B. & Grant, J. B. (2010). Digital dialogue? Australian politicians' use of the social network tool Twitter. *Australian Journal of Political Science*, 45(4), 579–604. doi: 10.1080/10361146.2010.517176

Greenwood, Justin. (1997). The succession of policy termination. *International Journal of Public Administration*, 20(12), 2121–2150.

Greer, C. F. & Ferguson, D. A. (2011). Using Twitter for promotion and branding: A content analysis of local television Twitter sites. *Journal of Broadcasting & Electronic Media*, 55(2), 198–214. doi: 10.1080/08838151.2011.570824

Greysen, S. R., Kind, T. & Chretien, K. C. (2010). Online professionalism and the mirror of social media. *Journal of General Internal Medicine*, 25(11), 1227–1229. doi: 10.1007/s11606-010-1447-1

Griggs, Steven & Howarth, David. (2008). Populism, localism and environmental politics: The logic and rhetoric of the stop stansted expansion campaign. *Planning Theory*, 7(2), 123–144.

Griggs, Steven & Howarth, David. (2011). Discourse and practice: Using the power of well being. *Evidence & Policy: A Journal of Research, Debate and Practice*, 7(2), 213–226.

Griggs, S. & Howarth, D. (2013). *The Politics of Airport Expansion in the United Kingdom: Hegemony, Policy and the Rhetoric of 'Sustainable Aviation'*. Manchester: University of Manchester Press.

Grint, Keith & Holt, Clare. (2011). Leading questions: If 'Total Place','Big Society'and local leadership are the answers: What's the question? *Leadership*, 7(1), 85–98.

Grundmann, Reiner & Krishnamurthy, Ramesh. (2010). The discourse of climate change: A corpus-based approach. *Critical Approaches to Discourse Analysis across Disciplines*, 4(2), 125–146.

Gruzd, A., Wellman, B. & Takhteyev, Y. (2011). Imagining Twitter as an imagined community. *American Behavioral Scientist*, 55(10), 1294–1318. doi: 10.1177/0002764211409378

Hackert, C. & Braehler, G. (2007). *FlashQ, version 1.0*. Retrieved from http.//www. hackert.biz/flashq, accessed 15 January 2011.

Hajer, Maarten A. (1995). *The Politics of Environmental Discourse: Ecological Modernization and the Policy Process*. Clarendon Press Oxford.

Hajer, Maarten A. (2010). *Authoritative Governance: Policy Making in the Age of Mediatization*. Oxford: Oxford University Press.

Hall, Peter A. (1989). The political power of economic ideas: Keynesianism across nations. Princeton, NJ: Princeton University Press.

Hanna, R., Rohm, A. & Crittenden, V. L. (2011). We're all connected: The power of the social media ecosystem. *Business Horizons*, 54(3), 265–273. doi: 10.1016/j.bushor.2011.01.007

Hansard. (2011). *House of Commons Hansard Debates for 28 February 2011 (pt 0004)*. Retrieved from http://www.publications.parliament.uk/pa/cm201011/cmhansrd/cm110228/debtext/110228-0004.htm.

Harzing, Anne-Wil & van der Wal, Ron. (2009). A Google Scholar h-index for journals: An alternative metric to measure journal impact in economics and business. *Journal of the American Society for Information Science and Technology*, 60(1), 41–46.

Hawn, C. (2009). Take two aspirin and tweet me in the morning: How Twitter, Facebook, and other social media are reshaping health care. *Health Affairs*, 28(2), 361–368. doi: 10.1377/hlthaff.28.2.361

Hay, Colin & Wincott, Daniel. (1998). Structure, agency and historical institutionalism. *Political Studies*, 46(5), 951–957.

Hilden A. H. (1958). Q-Sort correlation: Stability and random choice of statements. *Journal of Consulting Psychology*, 22(1), 45.

Hogwood, Brian W. & Peters, B., Guy. (1982). The dynamics of policy change: Policy succession. *Policy Sciences*, 14(3), 225–245.

Hong, S. M. (2012). Online news on Twitter: Newspapers' social media adoption and their online readership. *Information Economics and Policy*, 24(1), 69–74. doi: 10.1016/j.infoecopol.2012.01.004

Hopkins, Lewis D. & Zapata, Marisa A. (2007). *Engaging the Future: Forecasts, Scenarios, Plans, and Projects*. Phoenix: Lincoln Institute of Land Policy.

Hoppe, Robert. (2009). Scientific advice and public policy: Expert advisers' and policymakers' discourses on boundary work. *Poiesis & Praxis*, 6(3–4), 235–263.

Howarth, David. (2000). *Discourse*. Maidenhead: Open University Press.

Howarth, D., Norval, A. & Stavrakakis, Y. (eds.) (2000). *Discourse Theory and Political Analysis: Identities, Hegemonies and Social Change*. Manchester: Manchester University Press.

Howarth, David R. & Torfing, Jacob. (2005). *Discourse Theory in European Politics*. Basingstoke: Palgrave Macmillan.

Howson, Richard. (2007). From ethico-political hegemony to postmarxism. *Rethinking Marxism*, 19(2), 234–244. doi: 10.1080/08935690701219066

Hsu, C. L. & Park, H. W. (2012). Mapping online social networks of Korean politicians. *Government Information Quarterly*, 29(2), 169–181. doi: 10.1016/j.giq.2011.09.009

Hubbard, Douglas W. (2011). *Pulse: The New Science of Harnessing Internet Buzz to Track Threats and Opportunities*. Oxford: John Wiley & Sons.

Hudson, Jenny. (2002). Primary care lift is boost for GPs, *Birmingham Post*, 8 July.

Hull, B. (2012). Why can't we be 'Friends'? A call for a less stringent policy for judges using online social networking. *Hastings Law Journal*, 63(2), 595–631.

Hutchins, B. (2011). The acceleration of media sport culture Twitter, telepresence and online messaging. *Information Communication & Society*, 14(2), 237–257. doi: 10.1080/1369118x.2010.508534

Jeffares, Stephen. (2008). *Why Public Policy Ideas Catch On: Empty Signifiers and Flourishing Neighbourhoods*. University of Birmingham.

Jeffares, Stephen. (2014). Bedroom Tax Study at http://jeffar.es, accessed 28 February.

Jeffares, Stephen & Skelcher, Chris. (2011). Democratic subjectivities in network governance: AQ methodology study of English and Dutch public managers. *Public Administration*, 89(4), 1253–1273.

Junco, R., Heiberger, G. & Loken, E. (2011). The effect of Twitter on college student engagement and grades. *Journal of Computer Assisted Learning*, 27(2), 119–132. doi: 10.1111/j.1365-2729.2010.00387.x

Jungherr, A., Jurgens, P. & Schoen, H. (2012). Why the Pirate Party Won the German Election of 2009 or The Trouble With Predictions: A Response to Tumasjan, A., Sprenger, T. O., Sander, P. G., & Welpe, I. M. "Predicting Elections With Twitter: What 140 Characters Reveal About Political Sentiment". *Social Science Computer Review*, 30(2), 229–234. doi: 10.1177/0894439311404119

Kaplan, A. M. & Haenlein, M. (2010). Users of the world, unite! The challenges and opportunities of social media. *Business Horizons*, 53(1), 59–68. doi: 10.1016/j.bushor.2009.09.003

Kaplan, A. M. & Haenlein, M. (2011). The early bird catches the news: Nine things you should know about micro-blogging. *Business Horizons*, 54(2), 105–113. doi: 10.1016/j.bushor.2010.09.004

Kaplan, A. M. & Haenlein, M. (2012). The Britney Spears universe: Social media and viral marketing at its best. *Business Horizons*, 55(1), 27–31. doi: 10.1016/j.bushor.2011.08.009

Kasprzak, Emma. (2012). *BBC News – Social media and the PCC elections: Tweeting candidates*. Retrieved from http://www.bbc.co.uk/news/uk-england -19883502, accessed 22 June 2013.

Kettell, S. (2012). Thematic review religion and the Big Society: A match made in heaven? *Policy Polit.*, 40(2), 281–296.

Kim, Y., Huang, J. & Emery, S. (2013). *From the Known Knowns to the Unknown Unknowns: Precision and Relevance with Social Data*. Paper presented at the Big Data in Public Health Conference, Philadelphia, PA. Retrieved from http://www.healthmediacollaboratory.org/what-weve-learned/ presentations/, accessed 11 November 2013.

Kingdon, John W. (1995). *Agendas, Alternatives and Public Policies*. New York: HarperCollins College Publishers.

Klijn, Erik-Hans & Skelcher, Chris. (2007). Democracy and governance networks: Compatible or not? *Public Administration*, 85(3), 587–608.

Kroesen, Maarten & Bröer, Christian. (2009). Policy discourse, people's internal frames, and declared aircraft noise annoyance: An application of Q-methodology. *The Journal of the Acoustical Society of America*, 126, 195.

Lacan, Jacques. (1982). God and the jouissance of the woman. A love letter. *Feminine Sexuality.cmp*, 137–148.

Laclau, Ernesto. (2005). *The Populist Reason*. London: Verso.

Laclau, Ernesto & Mouffe, Chantal. (2001). *Hegemony and Socialist Strategy: towards a Radical Democratic Politics*. London: Verso.

Lariscy, R. W., Avery, E. J., Sweetser, K. D. & Howes, P. (2009). An examination of the role of online social media in journalists' source mix. *Public Relations Review*, 35(3), 314–316. doi: 10.1016/j.pubrev.2009.05.008

Larsson, A. O. & Moe, H. (2012). Studying political microblogging: Twitter users in the 2010 Swedish election campaign. *New Media & Society*, 14(5), 729–747. doi: 10.1177/1461444811422894

Lasorsa, D. L., Lewis, S. C. & Holton, A. E. (2012). Normalizing Twitter: Journalism practice in an emerging communication space. *Journalism Studies*, 13(1), 19–36. doi: 10.1080/1461670x.2011.571825

Lassen, D. S. & Brown, A. R. (2011). Twitter: The electoral connection? *Social Science Computer Review*, 29(4), 419–436. doi: 10.1177/0894439310382749

Lasswell, Harold D. (1949). Style in the language of politics. *Language of Politics: Studies in Quantitative Semantics (New York, 1949)*, 29, 31.

Lasuen, J. R. (1969). On growth poles. *Urban Studies*, 6(2), 137–161.

Lee, E. J. & Shin, S. Y. (2012). Are they talking to me? Cognitive and affective effects of interactivity in politicians' Twitter communication. *Cyberpsychology Behavior and Social Networking*, 15(10), 515–520. doi: 10.1089/cyber. 2012.0228

Lesniewksi, S. (2011). Letter, paying for Cameron's Big Society. 9th February 2011. The Guardian (newspaper – letter to the editor).

Lindgren, S. & Lundstrom, R. (2011). Pirate culture and hacktivist mobilization: The cultural and social protocols of #WikiLeaks on Twitter. *New Media & Society*, 13(6), 999–1018. doi: 10.1177/1461444811414833

Liu, Z. M., Liu, L. & Li, H. (2012). Determinants of information retweeting in microblogging. *Internet Research*, 22(4), 443–466. doi: 10.1108/ 10662241211250980

Local Leadership Centre. (2009). *Total Place*. Website: Date accessed 31 December 2009. Retrieved from http://www.localleadership.gov.uk/ totalplace/totalplaces/others/

LocalGov. (2010). *Government to Retain Principles of Total Place*. 10 June 2010. Retrieved from http://www.localgov.co.uk/index.cfm?method=news. detail&id=89149, accessed 14 January 2011.

Lotan, G., Graeff, E., Ananny, M., Gaffney, D., Pearce, I. & Boyd, D. (2011). The revolutions were Tweeted: Information flows during the 2011 Tunisian and Egyptian revolutions. *International Journal of Communication*, 5, 1375–1405.

Lovejoy, K. & Saxton, G. D. (2012). Information, community, and action: How nonprofit organizations use social media. *Journal of Computer-Mediated Communication*, 17(3), 337–353. doi: 10.1111/j.1083-6101.2012.01576.x

Lu, Chi-Jung & Shulman, Stuart W. (2008). Rigor and flexibility in computer-based qualitative research: Introducing the coding analysis toolkit. *International Journal of Multiple Research Approaches*, 2(1), 105–117.

Lyons, Michael. (2001). Perspective: Privileged to Join in Times of Pain and Joy, *Birmingham Post*. 29 September.

Malhotra, A., Malhotra, C. K. & See, A. (2012). How to get your messages retweeted. *Mit Sloan Management Review*, 53(2), 61.

Marwick, A. E. & Boyd, D. (2011). I tweet honestly, I tweet passionately: Twitter users, context collapse, and the imagined audience. *New Media & Society*, 13(1), 114–133. doi: 10.1177/1461444810365313

Mathur, N. & Skelcher, C. (2007). Evaluating democratic performance: Methodologies for assessing the relationship between network governance and citizens. *Public Administration Review*, 67(2), 228–237.

Mayer-Schönberger, V. & Cukier, K. U. (2013). *Big Data: A Revolution That Will Transform How We Live, Work, and Think*. Boston, MA: Houghton Mifflin Harcourt.

Methmann, Chris Paul. (2010). 'Climate protection' as empty signifier: A discourse theoretical perspective on climate mainstreaming in world politics. *Millennium-Journal of International Studies*, 39(2), 345–372.

Mirror, Daily. (2011). Big Society is a big con. *Daily Mirror*. 8th February.

Mitchell, Amy & Hitlin, Paul. (2013). *Twitter Reaction to Events Often at Odds with Overall Public Opinion*. Retrieved from http://www.pewresearch.org/2013/03/04/twitter-reaction-to-events-often-at-odds-with-overall-public-opinion/, accessed 22 June 2013.

Moe, H. (2012). Who participates and how? Twitter as an arena for public debate about the data retention directive in Norway. *International Journal of Communication*, 6, 1222–1244.

Moore, Mark H. (1990). What sort of ideas become public ideas? In R. B. Reich (ed.), *The Power of Public Ideas* (pp. 55–83). Cambridge, MA: Harvard University Press.

Mungiu-Pippidi, A. & Munteanu, I. (2009). Moldova's 'Twitter Revolution'. *Journal of Democracy*, 20(3), 136–142.

Muntinga, D. G., Moorman, M. & Smit, E. G. (2011). Introducing COBRAs exploring motivations for brand-related social media use. *International Journal of Advertising*, 30(1), 13–46. doi: 10.2501/ija-30-1-013-046

Muralidharan, S., Dillistone, K. & Shin, J. H. (2011). The Gulf Coast oil spill: Extending the theory of image restoration discourse to the realm of social media and beyond petroleum. *Public Relations Review*, 37(3), 226–232. doi: 10.1016/j.pubrev.2011.04.006

Mycock, A. & Tonge, J. (2011). A big idea for the Big Society? The advent of national citizen service. *Political Quarterly*, 82(1), 56–66.

Naaman, M., Becker, H. & Gravano, L. (2011). Hip and trendy: Characterizing emerging trends on Twitter. *Journal of the American Society for Information Science and Technology*, 62(5), 902–918. doi: 10.1002/asi.21489

Nanus, Burt. (1995). *Visionary Leadership: Creating a Compelling Sense of Direction for Your Organization*. San Francisco, CA: Jossey-Bass.

Needham, C. (2011). *Personalising Public Services: Understanding the Personalisation Narrative*. Bristol: Policy Press.

Neuhaus, F. & Webmoor, T. (2012). Agile ethics for massified research and visualization. *Information Communication & Society*, 15(1), 43–65. doi: 10.1080/1369118x.2011.616519

Newman, Janet. (2001). *Modernizing Governance: New Labour, Policy and Society*. London: SAGE.

Niemeyer, Simon, Petts, Judith & Hobson, Kersty. (2005). Rapid climate change and society: Assessing responses and thresholds. *Risk Analysis*, 25(6), 1443–1456.

Norman, M. (2012). Saturday night's alright for Tweeting: Cultural citizenship, collective discussion, and the new media consumption/production of hockey day in Canada. *Sociology of Sport Journal*, 29(3), 306–324.

NxtGen, M. C. & Gee, R. (2011). *Andrew Lansley Rap*. Retrieved from http://www.youtube.com/watch?v=Dl1jPqqTdNo, accessed 22 June 2013.

Obama, B. (2012). *Four more years*. Retrieved from https://twitter.com/BarackObama/status/266031293945503744 *Twitter*. Accessed 22 June 2013.

Ockwell, David G. (2008). 'Opening up' policy to reflexive appraisal: A role for Q methodology? A case study of fire management in Cape York, Australia. *Policy Sciences*, 41(4), 263–292. doi: 10.1007/s11077-008-9066-y

Offe, Claus. (2009). Governance: An 'Empty Signifier'? *Constellations*, 16(4), 550–562.

Oh, O., Agrawal, M. & Rao, H. R. (2011). Information control and terrorism: Tracking the Mumbai terrorist attack through Twitter. *Information Systems Frontiers*, 13(1), 33–43. doi: 10.1007/s10796-010-9275-8

Page, R. (2012). The linguistics of self-branding and micro-celebrity in Twitter: The role of hashtags. *Discourse & Communication*, 6(2), 181–201. doi: 10.1177/1750481312437441

Papacharissi, Z. & Oliveira, M. D. (2012). Affective news and networked publics: The rhythms of news storytelling on #Egypt. *Journal of Communication*, 62(2), 266–282. doi: 10.1111/j.1460-2466.2012.01630.x

Parent, M., Plangger, K. & Bal, A. (2011). The new WTP: Willingness to participate. *Business Horizons*, 54(3), 219–229. doi: 10.1016/j.bushor.2011.01.003

Parsons, D. W. (1995). *Public Policy: An Introduction to the Theory and Practice of Policy Analysis*. Cheltenham: Edward Elgar.

Partnership, Birmingham City Strategic. (2002). Neighbourhood Renewal Strategy for Birmingham. Birmingham: Birmingham City Council.

Pattie, Charles & Johnston, Ron. (2011). How big is the Big Society? *Parliamentary Affairs*, 64(3), 403–424.

Peters, B. Guy & Hogwood, Brian W. (1985). In search of the issue-attention cycle. *The Journal of Politics*, 47(01), 238–253.

Petter, John. (2005). Responsible behavior in bureaucrats: An expanded conceptual framework. *Public Integrity*, 7(3), 197–217.

Pollitt, Christopher & Hupe, Peter. (2011). Talking about government: The role of magic concepts. *Public Management Review*, 13(5), 641–658.

Post, Birmingham. (2001). Birmingham Post Comment: A City Renewed, Birmingham Post. *Birmingham Post,* 29 September 2001.

Prasad, Raghavendra S. (2001). Development of the HIV/AIDS Q-sort instrument to measure physician attitudes. *Family Medicine-Kansas City*, 33(10), 772–778.

Prateepko, Tapanan & Chongsuvivatwong, Virasakdi. (2009). Patterns of perception toward influenza pandemic among the front-line responsible health personnel in southern Thailand: A Q methodology approach. *BMC Public Health*, 9(1), 161.

Prochaska, J. J., Pechmann, C., Kim, R. & Leonhardt, J. M. (2012). Twitter quitter? An analysis of Twitter quit smoking social networks. *Tobacco Control*, 21(4), 447–449. doi: 10.1136/tc.2010.042507

Public Property. (2010). *Doubts Over Coalition Support for Total Place Scheme*. Retrieved from http://www.publicpropertyuk.com/2010/05/21/doubts-over-coalition-support-for-total-place-scheme/, accessed 11 January 2011.

Q Method (2013). *Q Methodology: A Method for Modern Research*. Retrieved from http://qmethod.org/links, accessed 22 June 2013.

Quinn, Robert E. (1991). *Beyond Rational Management: Mastering the Paradoxes and Competing Demands of High Performance*. San Francisco: Jossey-Bass.

Reich, Robert B. (ed.). (1990). *The Power of the Public Ideas*. Cambridge, MA: Harvard University Press.

Richardson, Jeremy. (2000). Government, interest groups and policy change. *Political Studies*, 48(5), 1006–1025.

Rogers, E. M. (2003). *Diffusion of Innovations*, 5th Edition. New York: Free Press.

Roosevelt, F. D. (1934). Fireside Chat: The Achievements of the 73rd Congress. http://docs.fdrlibrary.marist.edu/062834.html, accessed 1 March 2014.

Rowlands, I., Nicholas, D., Russell, B., Canty, N. & Watkinson, A. (2011). Social media use in the research workflow. *Learned Publishing*, 24(3), 183–195. doi: 10.1087/20110306

Rui, H. X. & Whinston, A. (2012). Information or attention? An empirical study of user contribution on Twitter. *Information Systems and E-Business Management*, 10(3), 309–324. doi: 10.1007/s10257-011-0164-6

Rutherford, Murray B., Gibeau, Michael L., Clark, Susan G. & Chamberlain, Emily C. (2009). Interdisciplinary problem solving workshops for grizzly bear conservation in Banff National park, Canada. *Policy Sciences*, 42(2), 163–187.

Schmidt, Vivien A. (2010). Taking ideas and discourse seriously: explaining change through discursive institutionalism as the fourth 'new institutionalism'. *European Political Science Review*, 2(1), 1–25.

Schmidt, Vivien A. & Radaelli, Claudio M. (2004). Policy change and discourse in Europe: Conceptual and methodological issues. *West European Politics*, 27(2), 183–210.

Schön, Donald A. (1963). *Invention and the Evolution of Ideas*. London: Tavistock Publications Ltd.

Serrano-Puche, J. (2012). Digital influence measurement tools: An analysis of Klout and PeerIndex. *Profesional De La Informacion*, 21(3), 298–303.

Shipley, Robert. (2000). The origin and development of vision and visioning in planning. *International Planning Studies*, 5(2), 225–236.

Shipley, Robert & Newkirk, Ross. (1999). Vision and visioning in planning: What do these terms really mean? *Environment and Planning B*, 26, 573–592.

Shulman, Stuart W. (2009). The case against mass E-mails: Perverse incentives and low quality public participation in US federal rulemaking. *Policy & Internet*, 1(1), 23–53.

Shulman, Stuart. (2011). DiscoverText: Software training to unlock the power of text. *Proceedings of the 12th Annual International Digital Government Research Conference: Digital Government Innovation in Challenging Times* (pp. 373–373): ACM.

Shulman, Stuart. (2012, 17 June 2013). *DiscoverText An Introduction to the Key Tools and Methods*. [Video] Retrieved from http://www.screencast.com/t/BtBDsBTtw

Silver, N. (2012). *The Signal and the Noise: Why So Many Predictions Fail-but Some Don't*. London: Penguin Group US.

Skelcher, Chris, Sullivan, Helen & Jeffares, Stephen (2013). *Hybrid Governance in European Cities: Neighbourhood, Migration and Democracy*. Palgrave Macmillan,

Small, T. A. (2011). What the Hashtag? A content analysis of Canadian politics on Twitter. *Information Communication & Society*, 14(6), 872–895. doi: 10.1080/1369118x.2011.554572, accessed 22 June 2013.

Smith, A. N., Fischer, E. & Chen, Y. J. (2012). How does brand-related user-generated content differ across YouTube, Facebook, and Twitter? *Journal of Interactive Marketing*, 26(2), 102–113. doi: 10.1016/j.intmar.2012.01.002

Smith, B. G. (2010). Socially distributing public relations: Twitter, Haiti, and interactivity in social media. *Public Relations Review*, 36(4), 329–335. doi: 10.1016/j.pubrev.2010.08.005

Smith, Craig. (2013). *By the Numbers: 16 Amazing Twitter Stats.* Retrieved from http://expandedramblings.com/index.php/march-2013-by-the-numbers-a-few-amazing-twitter-stats, accessed 22 June 2013.

Smith, Martin J. (2010). From big government to big society: Changing the state–society balance. *Parliamentary Affairs*, 63(4), 818–833.

Sreenivasan, N. D., Lee, C. S. & Goh, D. H. L. (2012). Tweeting the friendly skies Investigating information exchange among Twitter users about airlines. *Program-Electronic Library and Information Systems*, 46(1), 21–42. doi: 10.1108/00330331211204548

Stavrakakis, Yannis. (2012). *Lacan and the Political.* London: Routledge.

Steelman, Toddi & Maguire, Lynn A. (1999). Understanding participant perspectives: Q-methodology in national forest management. *Journal of Policy Analysis and Management*, 18(3), 361–388.

Stephenson, William. (1953). *The Study of Behavior: Q-technique and Its Methodology.* Chicago: University of Chicago Press.

Stephenson, William. (1978). Concourse theory of communication. *Communication*, 3, 21–40.

Stone, Diane. (1999). Learning lessons and transferring policy across time, space and disciplines. *Politics*, 19(1), 51–59.

Sullivan, Helen. (2012). Debate: A Big Society needs an active state. *Policy & Politics*, 40(1), 141–144.

Sutton, J. N. (2009). Social media monitoring and the democratic national convention: New tasks and emergent processes. *Journal of Homeland Security and Emergency Management*, 6(1), 22.

Szczypka, G., Emery, S. & Aly, E. (2012). Harvesting the Twitter firehose for measurement and analysis: A content analysis of tweets from the CDC's Tips from Former Smokers campaign. Paper presented at the National Conference on Health Communication, Marketing, and Media, Atlanta, GA. Retrieved from http://www.healthmediacollaboratory.org/wp-content/uploads/2012/11/Szczypka_hcmmconf2012.pdf, accessed 22 June 2013.

The Cabinet Office (2012). Social media guidance for civil servants, https://www.gov.uk/government/publications/social-media-guidance-for-civil-servants, accessed 26 June 2013.

Thelwall, M., Buckley, K. & Paltoglou, G. (2011). Sentiment in Twitter Events. *Journal of the American Society for Information Science and Technology*, 62(2), 406–418. doi: 10.1002/asi.21462

Thelwall, M., Buckley, K. & Paltoglou, G. (2012). Sentiment strength detection for the social web. *Journal of the American Society for Information Science and Technology*, 63(1), 163–173. doi: 10.1002/asi.21662

Thomas, Dan B. & Baas, Larry R. (1992). The issue of generalization in Q methodology: 'Reliable schematics' revisited. *Operant Subjectivity*, 16(1), 18–36.

Times. (2011). Editorial: The Shrinking Idea, the Big Society needs to be about more than voluntary action. *Times*, 2. 8 February 2011.

Torfing, Jacob. (1999). *New Theories of Discourse: Laclau, Mouffe and Zizek.* Wiley.

Torfing, Jacob. (2005). Discourse theory: Achievements, arguments, and challenges, in Howarth, D. & Torfing, J, (eds.) *Discourse Theory in European Politics: Identity, Policy and Governance*, Basingstoke: Palgrave Macmillan, 1–32.

Torres-Salinas, D. & Delgado-Lopez-Cozar, E. (2009). Strategies to improve the dissemination of research results with the Web 2.0. *Profesional De La Informacion*, 18(5), 534–539.

Toulmin, Stephen. (1958). *The Philosophy of Science* (Vol. 14). London: Genesis Publishing Pvt Ltd.

Treasury, H. M. (2009). *Financial Statement and Budget Report: Budget 2009: Building Britain's Future*. London: Stationery Office/TSO.

Treasury, H. M. (2010). *Total Place: A Whole Area Approach to Public Services*. London, HM Treasury.

Tumasjan, A., Sprenger, T. O., Sandner, P. G. & Welpe, I. M. (2011). Election forecasts with Twitter: How 140 characters reflect the political landscape. *Social Science Computer Review*, 29(4), 402–418. doi: 10.1177/0894439310386557

Tumasjan, A., Sprenger, T. O., Sander, P. G. & Welpe, I. M. (2011). Predicting elections with Twitter: What 140 characters reveal about political sentiment. *Social Science Computer Review*, 30(2), 229–234. doi: 10.1177/0894439310386557

van Eeten, Michel J. G. (2001). Recasting intractable policy issues: The wider implications of the Netherlands civil aviation controversy. *Journal of Policy Analysis and Management*, 20(3), 391–414.

van Exel, N. J. A., de Graaf, G. & Rietveld, P. (2011). I can do perfectly well without a car! *Transportation*, 38(3), 383–407. doi: 10.1007/s11116-010-9315-8

van Hulst, Merlijn. & Gerrits, Lasse. (2008). *Dream On: The Use of the Vision Concept for Governing Networks*. Paper presented at the EGPA conference, Rotterdam.

Venables, Dan, Pidgeon, Nick, Simmons, Peter, Henwood, Karen & Parkhill, Karen. (2009). Living with nuclear power: AQ-method study of local community perceptions. *Risk Analysis*, 29(8), 1089–1104.

Waters, R. D. & Jamal, J. Y. (2011). Tweet, tweet, tweet: A content analysis of nonprofit organizations' Twitter updates. *Public Relations Review*, 37(3), 321–324. doi: 10.1016/j.pubrev.2011.03.002

Waters, R. D., Tindall, N. T. J. & Morton, T. S. (2010). Media catching and the journalist-public relations practitioner relationship: How social media are changing the practice of media relations. *Journal of Public Relations Research*, 22(3), 241–264. doi: 10.1080/10627261003799202

Watts, S. & Stenner, P. (2012). *Doing Q Methodological Research: Theory, Method & Interpretation*. London: SAGE.

Whelan, James, Stone, Christopher, Lyons, Miriam, Wright, Natalie-Niamh, Long, Anna, Ryall, John & Harding-Smith, Rob. (2012). Big Society and Australia: How the UK government is dismantling the state and what it means for Australia. Sydney: Centre for Policy Development.

Wigley, S. & Lewis, B. K. (2012). Rules of engagement: Practice what you tweet. *Public Relations Review*, 38(1), 165–167. doi: 10.1016/j.pubrev.2011.08.020

Wilkinson, D. & Thelwall, M. (2012). Trending Twitter topics in English: An international comparison. *Journal of the American Society for Information Science and Technology*, 63(8), 1631–1646. doi: 10.1002/asi.22713

Williams, Raymond. (2013). *Keywords (Routledge Revivals): A Vocabulary of Culture and Society*. London: Routledge.

Willis, Martin & Jeffares, Stephen. (2012). Four viewpoints of whole area public partnerships. *Local Government Studies*, 38(5), 539–556.

Wolf, Amanda. (2004). The bones of a concourse. *Operant Subjectivity*, 27(3), 145–165.

Wolsink, M. (2004). Policy beliefs in spatial decisions: Contrasting core beliefs concerning space-making for waste infrastructure. *Urban Studies*, 41(13), 2669–2690. doi: 10.1080/0042098042000294619

Wong, William, Eiser, Arnold R., Mrtek, Robert G. & Heckerling, Paul S. (2004). By-person factor analysis in clinical ethical decision making: Q methodology in end-of-life care decisions. *The American Journal of Bioethics*, 4(3), W8–W22.

Wullweber, Joscha. (2008). Nanotechnology an empty signifier à venir? *Science, Technology & Innovation Studies*, 4(1).

Xifra, J. & Grau, F. (2010). Nanoblogging PR: The discourse on public relations in Twitter. *Public Relations Review*, 36(2), 171–174. doi: 10.1016/j.pubrev.2010.02.005

Youmans, W. L. & York, J. C. (2012). Social media and the activist toolkit: User agreements, corporate interests, and the information infrastructure of Modern Social Movements. *Journal of Communication*, 62(2), 315–329. doi: 10.1111/j.1460-2466.2012.01636.x

Zappavigna, M. (2011). Ambient affiliation: A linguistic perspective on Twitter. *New Media & Society*, 13(5), 788–806. doi: 10.1177/1461444810385097

Index

GPSR Compliance
The European Union's (EU) General Product Safety Regulation (GPSR) is a set
of rules that requires consumer products to be safe and our obligations to
ensure this.

If you have any concerns about our products, you can contact us on

ProductSafety@springernature.com

In case Publisher is established outside the EU, the EU authorized
representative is:

Springer Nature Customer Service Center GmbH
Europaplatz 3
69115 Heidelberg, Germany